Secrets For Higher Success

by

Vernon Howard

Previous Title

The Power of Psycho-Pictography

The Cosmic Key to the Inner Mind

New Life Foundation

www.anewlife.org

New Life Foundation
PO Box 2230
Pine AZ 85544

ISBN 0-911203-50-8

ABOUT VERNON HOWARD

****

Vernon Howard broke through to another world. He saw through the illusion of suffering and fear and loneliness. From 1965 until his death in 1992 he wrote books and conducted classes which reflect a degree of skill and understanding that may be unsurpassed in modern history. Tape recordings of many of his class talks are available.

Today more than 8 million readers worldwide enjoy his exceptionally clear and inspiring presentations of the great truths of the ages. His books are widely used by doctors, psychiatrists, psychologists, counselors, clergymen, educators and people from all walks of life. All his teachings center around the one grand theme: *"There is a way out of the human problem and anyone can find it."*

OTHER WRITINGS BY VERNON HOWARD

****

Psycho-Pictography
A Treasury of Trueness
The Power of Esoterics
Pathways to Perfect Living
Treasury of Positive Answers
Mystic Path to Cosmic Power
50 Ways to See Thru People
Be Safe in a Dangerous World
Your Power of Natural Knowing
50 Ways to Get Help from God
700 Inspiring Guides to a New Life
Women—50 Ways to See Thru Men
Conquer Anxiety and Frustration
Practical Exercises for Inner Harmony
And Many Others

CONTENTS

12. How the Inspired Life Comes to You

How This Book Can Change and Refresh Your Life

Throughout history, unhappy man has asked himself two baffling questions:

"Is there a way out?"

"If so, can I find it?"

The esoteric principles of this book reply:

"Yes, there is a way out."

"Yes, you can personally find it."

Stories and anecdotes have been the teaching tools of the great instructors and philosophers throughout the ages. Stories serve as clear channels by which life-transforming truths flow gently into the receptive mind, to heal and refresh. Some of the stories in this book are based on historical fact, including "The Awakening of George Fox" and "Socrates and the Nobleman." Others come from ancient legends or from esoteric schools, such as schools of Zen and Sufism and Taoism. But all the stories have the same aim—to lead each man to a higher place within himself.

What do we mean by esotericism? We mean those truths which enable a man or a woman to *think and act in a totally new way.* We mean those unique and truly practical principles which change the interior nature of whoever invites them into his daily life. With such an invitation a man unites his inner powers under a single flag, giving him conquest over fear, confusion and over every other unwanted condition.

This book includes questions by men and women who are adventuring toward the top of the mountain. The answers given to them are additional lights for your own path.

Read these pages casually, easily, yet alertly. See the deeper meanings in both the story and in the discussion which follows each story. Then you will know what life is all about, and you will know from your own independent intelligence.

You will know there is a way out because you have found it for yourself.

Vernon Howard

1

You Can Discover a Miraculous World

THE PEOPLE ON THE MOUNTAIN

There was once a village which was located in the desert at the bottom of a mountain. Its inhabitants had never known any other place to live. Their chief product was a series of small wooden idols which they manufactured from the dry bushes of the area. They placed great value on their idols, proudly displaying them wherever possible. They spent considerable time trying to lure strangers into town in order to convert them to their idol-making way of life.

One day they were surprised to hear that a small group of people lived on top of the mountain above their town. They had always believed it impossible to live in such a high place. But deciding to try to sell their idols to these strangers, they sent their most persuasive salesmen up the mountain path. But when the idols were displayed, the mountain people showed no interest at all, which shocked and angered the desert people. The idol-salesmen tried to argue, but the strangers declined argumentation also. One of the mountain men politely explained, "We have our own valuable items up here. They are natural, not manufactured. They are made from a precious element we call gold. Would you like to hear about it?"

Never having heard of gold, the desert dwellers glared suspiciously at the men whom they now considered to be enemies. Each salesman burned with the thought, "By rejecting our idols they also reject us." So in hostility and fear, they descended the mountain, burdened by their heavy stock of goods. The first thing they did was to hysterically spread lies about the mountain people, and to warn everyone against the strange product called gold.

But every once in a while, certain desert dwellers felt intensely dissatisfied with being desert dwellers, so they climbed the mountain path to investigate for themselves. Sensing something right and honest about the mountain people, they became mountain people themselves.

The path to self-awakening

Where does the path start? It starts with *something totally different*. Now, this something different cannot be pictured by the surface mind, for anything which can be pictured comes out of memory, and is therefore not different, but already familiar. If you know one tree when you see one, you will know a second tree, even though it is of another variety. Where does this leave us? Exactly where we must always be—in a position of receptivity to the unknown. To make a new guest welcome, we must stand aside from the doorway.

So the path starts with the resolve to think from an originally pure mind, not from society's conditioning. English mystic William Blake declared, "I must create my own system or be enslaved by another man's." A child who becomes personally aware that two and two add up to four will never permit a thousand other children to convince him that they add up to six. His personal knowledge of rightness exposes wrongness whenever it appears. Likewise, when we are our own rightness, we are no man's dupe.

The awakened man sees society's problems in an entirely different way from the social authorities who are called upon to solve the problems. Seeing their source in confused human nature, he knows the only cure is in individual self-awakening. He knows there can be no mass cure, for the masses do not want cure; they want the ego-excitement provided by social chaos. What is vital is for you to see this for yourself.

Roger Y. listened attentively as the preceding ideas were discussed in a class session. During the question period he asked, "I want to climb this mountain you speak about, but confusion seems so inevitable for people." Response: "Inevitable for whom? You must always speak about an individual, not about men and women in general. Confusion need not be inevitable for any individual who prefers clarity."

Like all men who were determined to do their own thinking, French philosopher Blaise Pascal was baffled at first over the correct way to rely upon his own mind. He decided upon a single, simple and effective method, which eventually served him with deep wisdom. The method was to carefully submit every theory to the judgment of his own internal nature.

Just as you do not mentally accept every piece of music you hear, you must not accept every idea coming your way, but must see whether it falls in tune with your true nature. Your own awakening essence is perfectly capable of distinguishing between imitation life and the free life you really want to live.

THE AWAKENING OF GEORGE FOX

From his earliest years, George Fox, the English spiritual leader, wanted to know what life was all about. Observing the deceit and cruelty and suffering of the world around him, he wondered whether there might be another way to live. So like Socrates and Plato before him, Fox sought the help of those who were supposed to know the answers, including the publicly prominent scholars and educators. While earning his living in wool and cattle, he spent every spare minute trying to crack open the mystery of human distress, including his own.

Fox was shocked into self-awakening from the very start. On one occasion he called upon a teacher who was noted for his great learning and fine character. While discussing spiritual matters, the two men walked in the scholar's garden. Fox accidentally stepped on the flower bed, "at which the man was in such a rage as if his house had been on fire. Thus all our discourse was lost, and I went away in sorrow."

Another lecturer, impressed by some ideas Fox had expressed during a conversation, soon used them in one of his sermons, leaving Fox dismayed. A third teacher gossiped to others about private information Fox had given him. The astonished and disappointed seeker wrote, "They did not possess what they professed," and "I saw they were all miserable comforters."

Later, when discarding everything but his own wish to find the true life, Fox found it. He declared triumphantly, "All things were new."

Eight steps toward a new life

George Fox is representative of those who have found their way out of the human jungle. Successful men and women have passed through the same experiences, and in the following order:

1. A deep, personal confusion and anguish.
2. A wish and a search for something different.
3. False trails, disappointments, increasing anguish.
4. Disillusionment with those who offer their help.
5. The first hint that careful self-study is the right start.
6. Shocking but healthy information about the inner person.
7. Gradual but steady self-awakening.
8. The fading away of confusion and anguish.

That which is not of our habitual nature has power to cure our habitual nature, and is always ready to do so, whether we call it God, Truth, Reality, Cosmic Energy or anything else.

When we know the facts from ourselves we no longer fall victim to society's distortions which parade around as facts.

We then see clearly that what is stated as the truth is not the truth at all, but something which contrives to please both the speaker and his listeners. It is quite possible for you to take your commands from within, rather than from shallow impressions coming from the outside world. In this happy state you will not be someone who subtracts from psychic health, but one who adds to it.

The human situation is a strange one. Consider the following example. People wonder how higher truths can possibly be of practical help in home or office, never once sensing that higher truths *alone* can help.

Higher thinking is truly magnificent, for insight into one difficulty can free you of a thousand other difficulties. Lila E. feared the displeasure of a certain person whom she depended upon for her sense of security. Studying the situation carefully, she saw how the other person sensed her dependency and took cruel advantage of it. This insight shook her loose from dependency in general, making her inwardly free from that particular person and from several other people.

An interesting change always occurs in the mind of those who persist along the path of higher principles. Their earlier steps were taken with shyness, uncertainty, with nervous glances at the unknown path ahead. Then, little by little, shyness was replaced by a new kind of boldness and good cheer, based on an inner certainty which no outside influence could shake. So even unexpected turns in the path are welcomed, for they know there are surprises but no dangers along this right path.

THE COCONUT TREE

A schoolteacher in Hawaii took her class on a nature hike. Her aim was to teach her pupils to observe carefully, to see everything there was to see about a natural object. She wanted them to go beyond surface conclusions to see the deeper facts.

When coming to a grove of coconut trees, she asked the class to study one tree very carefully. A few minutes later she asked, "Now, what do you know about the coconut tree? In how many ways does it supply man's needs?"

"It gives us food," said one pupil.

"Dried branches can be used for fuel," said another student.

"I have seen baskets woven out of the stems," said a third pupil, after which the class fell silent.

"The coconut palm is one of the most useful trees on earth," the teacher informed them. "So look again. Think about what you see."

After a few minutes of fresh observation, the encouraged pupils spoke up once more.

"The shells can be made into ornaments."

"The shops in town sell fans made of coconut leaves."

"Furniture can be built out of the trunk."

"I just remembered," exclaimed an enthusiastic boy, "that coconut oil comes from coconuts!"

Why you must be disillusioned

To observe, to explore, to think, to comprehend—that must be our aim. There is no beauty like the beauty of a person who truly wants to know what life is all about.

You must study your daily life just as carefully as you study these higher psychologies. They are not separate. Perhaps you observe an angry man. Also see that inwardly he is a weeping man, for anger and distress always go together. Maybe you feel upset because your request to another was denied. Study why you needed to make the request, for that will weaken its hold upon you. True spirituality is nothing more than to go about your daily affairs with a watchful mind.

One particular insight does marvels for your peace of mind toward unfolding daily events. It is the insight that everything happens as it must happen because of man's present low psychological level. Neither an individual nor society as a whole can possibly behave better than the level they occupy; they can only appear to do so. This insight replaces irritation and impatience with calmness and understanding. A mature mind knows that a small child cannot eat or dress more carefully than his present age permits.

The person who knows his inner world will also understand the outer world, and he can never be hurt by it.

Every incoming idea must be tested in the laboratory of personal experience. Perhaps someone tells you that self-satisfaction comes by involvement in exciting activities. If you sense discontent beneath your exciting activities, what you heard was all wrong. Maybe you read that men and events cannot frighten the enlightened man. If you experience this freedom in even a small way at first, what you read was certainly right. This is what is known as living from yourself.

Perhaps you say, as do many people, "But I am too disillusioned with life to look for a new way." Listen! You *must* be disillusioned with life, for it is the first step toward newness. Look around at self-satisfied people, sunning themselves in their successes, with concealed vanity. The truth can never reach such people, for it comes only to the ready, and disillusionment makes you ready. But at this point it is vital to channel your energies toward seeking the light, not toward condemning the darkness.

Maintain a steadfast confidence in your own abilities for self-transformation. If you are capable of one right action—which you are—you are also capable of a thousand right actions. There is no mystery about the source of strength for doing what must be done. Honesty is power. Simplicity is energy. Innocence is ability.

Charles F. said he wanted to let these higher principles change his way of living, but wondered about his abilities as a student. Anyone with similar self-doubt can be helped by hearing the reply which aided Charles: "You may not fully understand what you hear at first, but that is unimportant; just be interested in understanding. Remain interested in self-enlightenment and good things will happen."

THE CORRECTED DREAM

As his first move in building a new home, a man bought several acres of land in the country.

On his weekends he drove out to the country to prepare the ground for the actual building. Rocks were removed and the earth was leveled. Wild bushes and weeds were replaced with trees and flowers. The work was long and hard, but he felt richly rewarded by his dream of a new home in a pleasant atmosphere.

One afternoon, while hard at work, a real estate agent drove up with a puzzled look on his face. The agent asked the man whether he had been hired to improve the property, which brought a negative answer. Setting down his rake, the man identified himself as the owner of the land. Walking to his car, the agent returned with some papers which proved that the man was not the owner of the property he was working on. Through some mistake in paperwork, he was on the acres located next to his own, therefore he had not done a single thing to improve his property.

The man took the mistake in good spirits, made sure he was on his own land, and once more set about to make his dream come true.

What to do when humiliated

This story contains a lesson of extraordinary value to whoever wants to do something for himself. One reason why a man fails to reverse his inner direction is because he is required to acknowledge his present error. And the idea of admitting he has done nothing for himself over the years is a shock to his psychic system. But nothing is more courageous or more rewarding. Whoever finds he has been working on ground other than his own should not feel dismayed, to the contrary, he should feel delighted to be working for himself at last. What is wrong ground? Any attraction which distracts us from self-awareness.

"I admit," said Earl D. after his fifth class session, "the newness of your teaching, but I wish it was not so humiliating." Response: "Don't you see? It is precisely because it does humiliate you that it has value. It no longer permits you to play it safe —so you think—behind your walls of hardened thought. Humiliation forces you to see the folly of hiding from reality. Think about this one point for the next twenty-four hours."

Whenever a person or an event humiliates you, forget the outer happening and look at your humiliation. There is where the pain exists, and no amount of blaming outside factors will relieve the pain. This is where most people blunder. By blaming the exterior event they merely trade the pain of humiliation for the pain of anger. You might as well trade an attacking lion for a tiger. To get rid of both lion and tiger, remain completely humiliated, without fighting, for this destroys something unnecessary in you. This destruction is your deliverance.

Epictetus was one of those awakened men who made rich discoveries in the invisible world. Once a slave in an ancient Roman household, he was later set free, which permitted him to set up a school of philosophy in Nicopolis. Epictetus had the perfect answer for applicants who wondered whether they were ready for the great inner adventure: "When a man tells you that you know nothing, and you are not angry at him, you may be sure that you have begun to work."

Anything we want to understand can be understood, providing we start with the clear and honest awareness that we do not at present understand.

Consider the words "seriously" and "lightly". In higher thinking, these are not opposites, but the natural and productive way of meeting everything. It means to meet every event of life with a deep thoughtfulness which does not include negativity. A man might think seriously toward a loss of some kind, but by resenting the loss he robs himself of also thinking lightly, which could have produced peaceful understanding. To think seriously-lightly means to meet everything with a new mind, a mind without hardened judgments formed by past experiences. Experiment with this. Today, take everything seriously-lightly.

ESCAPE FROM THE FOREST

In order to illustrate right action leading to self-liberty, a teacher told the following story:

"Self-release can be compared to a man who has been kidnapped and carried away to a remote forest. While his kidnappers huddle around a fire a short distance away, he studies his situation. Feeling the tight ropes around his arms and legs, he realizes that escape will call for all his energy and intelligence. He manages to slip out of one rope, enabling him to stand upright. After inching forward a few inches, he loosens a second rope, then a third. Keeping as quiet as possible, he falls forward, picks himself up and falls forward again. He does not mind the falls and failures, for he sees them as part of his forward movement. Little by little, all his ropes become loose and fall away. Finally, he reaches the road which leads to home and liberty."

How to understand life

We can examine a specific condition which has captured millions of men and women, but which can be escaped through right action.

Barbara E. freely admitted, "Life often seems to have no meaning for me. In a corner of their minds, I think most people feel this. May I have your comment?" Reply: "The problem occurs because we try to impose our acquired meaning on to life. A man who fails to win what society calls success will think life meaningless, but he misses the point entirely. Let life have *its* meaning, which is true success. This is achieved by bravely abandoning memorized opinions about the nature of success. Think deeply about just this much. It will help unfold the entire picture."

There are many ways to describe our inner task. One of them is to call it a daring adventure in seeing what our habitual nature refuses to see. For example, many people decline to examine self-liberty, for fear it will rob them of what they believe are their enjoyments. But they fail to see how their excitements alternate with depressions, how their hopes are shoved aside by frustrations. No one is asked to give up enjoyment; he is asked to abandon his false concept of enjoyment, so that true refreshment may enter every moment.

What is the true feeling which is ours wherever we may find ourselves and whatever the task which occupies the mind and hand? It is a feeling of self-warmth which does not succumb to the coldness of social and physical environment. It is an inspiration without argument, without an impulse to stir up something in order to excite itself. It is pure feeling in which you relax completely, effortlessly, for you sense that you are both the feeling and the spontaneous source of the feeling.

Think of yourself as needing only the right connection in order to refresh your life. There is a lake of pure water in the mountain, but no one down on the prairie can be refreshed until a connecting channel is built. Marvin W. saw how tension decreased whenever he stopped insisting that he was right about everything. That was a healthy connection. Start making right connections for yourself.

Many business firms conduct a program in which they encourage suggestions from employees for improving daily efficiency. The offered suggestions often result in saving considerable time and money and energy. Make it a regular part of your inner work to suggest ways for psychic promotion. One day you might seek to understand why human beings cling to their self-defeating behavior. The next day you could refuse to be influenced by negative behavior in other people. The third day you might be cheered by realizing that every coin of self-knowledge earns interest from the moment of deposit.

Excellence in inner work does not mean the ability to move mountains, but a patient, cheerful, day by day application of what has been absorbed thus far. What may now appear to be an impassable obstruction will eventually be as nothing, for an eagle which can fly over a boulder can also fly over a mountain.

THE MAN WHO SAW HIMSELF

The owner of a large estate went out one night with a flashlight to make sure that everything was quietly settled down for the night. Assuring himself that everything was normal in the nearby grounds, he walked out to lock the front gate. Absorbed in his own thoughts, he failed to remember a recently dug ditch, into which he fell. Dazed and muddy, he continued to wander around, not quite sure of where he was or what he was doing. Pointing his flashlight at the various buildings and at the silent livestock, he saw them quite clearly in the light, but could not remember what connection they had with him.

After wandering around for a couple of hours, he began to sense that something was wrong with what he was doing. Dimly, he felt the futility of his pointless strayings. Also, he felt a strange rebellion against the bruises he suffered every time he bumped into an object which his flashlight failed to reveal.

It then occurred to him that while the flashlight could reveal various exterior objects, he himself was in darkness. So turning the light on himself, he saw with shock his actual condition of bruises and mud. Now seeing himself as he really was, he also knew what he must do for himself, which he did promptly. He returned home, where his injuries were dressed, and where his mental clearness returned.

A great secret of the ages

"You emphasize the necessity of simply *seeing,*" said Gerald T., "but I am not clear on what we are trying to see." Reply: "You are striving to see that a way of life exists which is above human conflict, above wondering what to do with yourself, above financial anxieties, above stabbing uncertainties, above frantic attempts to feel secure. This way exists."

Just as our blinking eyelids clear the eyes, so do truths like the following keep our inner vision clear and sharp:

1. If you really know yourself, you know all men.
2. We can either use a catastrophe or let a catastrophe use us.
3. There is a cause of fear but no reason for it.

4. You need only come home to yourself.
5. A present moment of awareness has total power over the last fifty years.
6. Do not compare and you cannot be unhappy.

The answer to a question resides at a higher level of understanding than the question. To remember this saves useless search. A fifth-grade child who asks a question of a friend at the next desk will get a fifth-grade answer. A sixth-grade answer can be obtained only by asking a pupil in the sixth grade. The inquiring child may not understand it at first, but its rightness will eventually come to him. In our spiritual schooling, daily promotion comes to the student who really wants to know.

Extremely difficult questions have extremely simple answers, if only we wish to hear them. People ask, "How come everything I do for myself really does nothing for me?" The answer is, we cannot trade our artificial gold for real money. Talking about love does not give the talker a feeling of love. We can learn what gold really is by asking with intense interest, "What is gold?" Then, when setting ourselves aside, we hear the answer.

The word "hiding" is an excellent starting point for self-exploration. First, we hide our inner negativities from ourselves and from others. For some strange reason we think it wiser to hide heartache than to examine it. Then, the very hiding of our anxiety is what blocks the abundance of health and happiness which could come with the successful exploration of anxiety. We hide from our own wholeness! We are like an heir to a fortune who never knows about it because he is hiding out in the woods in a frantic attempt to escape social poverty.

"Learn from conscious conflict!" Here is one of the great secrets of the ages. What does it mean? Mrs. Green fears rejection. By becoming calmly conscious of the entire process, the word "rejection" loses its meaning to her. Mr. Grey frantically battles others to win public prominence. By consciousness of the folly of public praise he turns toward inner riches. Miss White wearily plays a role of confidence which she does not feel. By becoming conscious of her tiring performance she learns to be a real person. *Learn from conscious conflict!*

Once you have joined yourself with a true and good thought, it is impossible to ever lose it. When you have gone beyond merely thinking about a truth to actually becoming one with that truth, that oneness is eternal. The truth is the state of the universe, and the universe cannot lose itself. Now you know why a student of higher knowledge is always accompanied by good cheer.

A HELPFUL SUMMARY OF CHAPTER ONE

1. Remember, you are exploring something totally new.
2. Self-awakening is our true adventure in life.
3. Confusion toward yourself is completely unnecessary.

4. To think from your own essence is to think profitably.
5. The magnificent cure is ready whenever we are ready.
6. Only these higher principles are truly practical.
7. Explore and absorb these teachings everyday.
8. Let life reveal its authentic meaning to you.
9. A life exists for you which is above human chaos.
10. This is the way of constant good cheer.

2

Sources of Help That Succeed Perfectly

THE MAGIC GLASS

A king heard that the citizens in one of his villages were fighting among themselves. In one way or another, everyone was hurting his neighbor. Wishing happiness for his people, the king sent a special messenger to the village with a Magic Glass. Whoever would look through the Magic Glass would see things as they were in reality, not according to illusion or imagination. So such viewers always became good and sensible and happy human beings.

The special messenger left the Magic Glass with the people, while knowing exactly what would happen, for he had been on such trips before.

One group of villagers gave the glass a name and worshipped it just as if it were a human being.

Others declared, "We already see things as they are, so what is the use of this glass?"

A third group refused to even come close to the glass for fear it would disturb their usual ways.

Other citizens stated, "The Magic Glass is fairly interesting, but we can't see how it can contribute to our daily needs in a practical world."

A few of the villagers changed themselves by actually looking through the Magic Glass. But most of the people went on fighting and hurting each other.

Turn on your inner light

You can take it as a fact that this Magic Glass consists of esoteric wisdom, of higher knowledge, of natural thinking. Before looking into some specific wisdoms, we can examine another phase of the preceding story.

Do not assume that a massive outpouring of people for a particular cause indicates the presence of rightness in their cause. We must not confuse a similarity in psychic sickness with unity of minds, for they have nothing in common. Fifty patients in a hospital with the same illness are still individually ill, and can help neither themselves nor others. The larger the crowd, the greater the hysteria and mindlessness.

A study of the psychology of crowds should be a mighty inducement for true individuality. Philip Sidney wrote, "Eagles fly alone; they are but sheep which always herd together." Ralph Waldo Emerson adds, "I wish to be a true and free man."

For today's exploration, take a familiar fact and try to peer very deeply into it. For example, you know that only the inner state is important, not outer appearances. Total insight into this will bring you into perfect tune with yourself. Do you see how it works? We feel our life according to the way we really think, not as we say we think or think we think. So by observing a contradiction between inner and outer behavior, we see the cause of self-conflict, which makes us want to end it.

Think of negative feelings as unhealthy vibrations which tear you apart, for that is just what they do. Watch for yourself how dejection or dismay shakes you back and forth, never providing a platform for stability. These vibrations provide a false feeling of life, which deceives millions. Those who are tired of being deceived will find the platform which exists above these vibrations.

A psychologist said, "I have noticed how many of my patients go wrong by enjoying what you call a false feeling of life. Will you please explain this a bit more?" Reply: "It is very easy to explain. Whoever prefers the false thrill of his anger, either open or concealed, cannot possess the healthy feeling which comes with the absence of anger. We get what we choose. The same applies to any other unhealthy state, including the false thrill of jealousy or scorn."

There is a light within us which is capable of extinguishing immediately any kind of disturbing darkness. In order to turn on this light we must love it more than we love the false feeling of life provided by darkness. For instance, we must not love the thrill of feeling persecuted. When we see—when we truly see—what darkness does to us, its false appeal fades away. Read once more the first sentence of this paragraph.

IN THE FLOWER GARDEN

In studying his students, an awakened man of a Zen school saw where many of them were going wrong. A large number of the pupils still believed in familiar but useless spiritual practices. For example, many of them gullibly believed that exterior religious ceremonies had power to transform their inner nature.

One afternoon, while with his pupils in the school's flower garden, the teacher saw his opportunity to make correction. Picking up a brick, he began to rub it with dramatic motions of his hand. The curious students gathered around. One student asked what was going on, to which the teacher replied, "I wish to make a mirror."

The student protested, "But no amount of rubbing a brick can turn it into a mirror."

The teacher made his point, "And no amount of

indulgence in exterior religious dramatics will awaken you to a new destiny."

Living in tension is unnecessary

This story carries a practical lesson for life-correction: "No amount of exterior appearances of rightness can ever make human beings feel right." There are only a few truly wise men in the world who see this deeply. They see clearly how human chaos is caused by human pretense. In contrast to these few, there are millions of men who try to appear wise by merely rearranging the disastrous effects of human deception.

One of the most difficult facts for human beings to see is that it is a thousand times better to spend one minute in attaining authentic inner goodness than to spend twenty years in exterior acts of goodness. But that is what we must see, and when we do, a great relief is ours.

Ibn Hazm, a Moslem scholar, spent most of his life trying to discover man's motives for doing what he did. His persistent inquiry brought him to this conclusion: "I have found only one motive—the need to escape anxiety."

A man anxiously asks, "If business slows down, how badly will it threaten my financial security?" and "What will happen to my peace of mind if my children get into trouble?" The next day he worries, "What can I do about my awful feeling of loneliness and isolation?" and "Why must I live in the fear that every move will be a new blunder bringing instant punishment?" But what if this man sees that he is not the "I" and the "me" he thinks he is? Would that not change his entire life? It would. This is why nothing is more vital than to end the false sense of self.

The story is told of a soldier who was ordered to stand solitary guard over a jungle trail. He expected to be relieved in a few hours, but had to endure the tension of a possible enemy attack for two days. It developed that someone had forgotten to tell him it was no longer necessary to guard the trail. Maybe you have never been told it is unnecessary to guard the ideas about yourself which make up what you call "I". Maybe you do not know of your liberty to walk away from your supposed duty any time you like. Know it now. Know of your rightful freedom to live without tense self-protection.

One of the richest truths ever spoken is, "Have the courage to lose what you call yourself and you will find yourself."

When a man begins to doubt the accuracy of his present ways of thinking, he should continue his doubt by observing the daily results of his present thinking. That is intelligence in action. When noticing the sour fruits in his day he should trace them back to his own habitual thought-patterns. The bright idea then occurs to him, "Since I have made my past days what they have been, I can also make future days what I truly wish them to be."

What would you think of a man who was hungry for a complete dinner but ate only the salad? His hunger would remain, just as people remain hungry by trying to live from only one part of themselves. We must feel life as well as think it. We must add listening to our talking. We must use disappointment instead of avoiding it. Wholeness comes by living wholly. Methods for releasing our energies fully are provided in Chapter Nine.

"It is unquestionably true," said Leslie L., "that an intelligent man uses everything in his day for self-insight, but how can we use those vague and haunting feelings which invade every moment of our day? We can't even identify them, but there they are, haunting our life." Reply: "People think they are haunted by life, when in fact they are haunted by what they have substituted for life. If you will understand this, your life will change in the way you want."

THE SCIENTIST WHO WON A MANSION

In reward for outstanding services, a country gave a scientist a beautiful and spacious mansion. But it was a rule in this country that every man had to earn even his own reward, so the scientist was told, "Your mansion contains fifty rooms. The door to each room has its own special lock, which you must solve. When you gain entrance to a room, study its contents carefully, then return to the city where a judge will hear your description of what you saw. When the judge sees that you are well acquainted with one room, you may go on to the next room. When you have knowledge of the entire mansion, it becomes your own."

Accepting the challenge, the scientist poured all

his skill into the task of unlocking one room at a time and becoming aware of its contents. By this patient work he learned all about the entire mansion, which was then turned over to him.

Twenty thoughts for self-wholeness

Like that scientist, we must proceed as if much depends upon our diligence—for it does. As psychic scientists we can approach each new thought with an intention to make it contribute to our wholeness, to make it mean something in everyday life. We want it to make us conscious and calm when others are confused and panicky, to keep us in health when society insists upon injuring itself. You will achieve these two aims, plus many others, by taking a deep interest in the following thoughts:

1. The New Life exists as a fact, whether we feel its existence or not, so if we remain faithful to the fact, we will finally feel it.
2. When full understanding comes to a man, such things as betrayal and disgrace and failure do not exist to him.
3. In one way or another, everyone you meet tries to make you the same as he is, so observe carefully the kind of life he leads.
4. We pass beyond loneliness by understanding it, after which we no longer trade our integrity for social trinkets, which means the end of troublesome involvements.
5. When first daring to drop a wrong idea we

anxiously feel as if we are losing part of ourselves, when, in fact, we are losing an imposter who kept us afraid.

6. If we think we understand ourselves, but do not, we will also think we understand others, but will not, which is why human relations are so disastrous.
7. When living correctly with yourself you will know exactly how to live in right relationship with others.
8. The path calls for sternness, not the sternness found in fear and anger, but the kind which refuses compromise because it knows at last the direction of the Treasure.
9. There is a great difference between the charm of mere surface personality and the charm of living from Truth.
10. Notice how people and events now drain you of energy, then notice how something in you objects to it, then use these principles to keep your own energy for yourself, which is not selfishness.
11. It is a magic moment when these truths are reflected upon not from a sense of duty but from a feeling of affection.
12. People always assume that freedom consists in getting something desirable from the exterior world, when in fact it consists exclusively of getting rid of something undesirable in the interior world.

13. We can be sure of many things regarding self-exploration, and none is more sure than its contribution to human sanity.
14. Instead of anxiously craving rewards, let cosmic principles change your idea of what it means to be rewarded, for beyond human rewards is the True Reward.
15. Sentimentality is bad because it includes too much of our unseen selves, but a simple affection without self-reference is good.
16. It is good to work with others on these ideas, but remain faithful to your inner task, never permitting a pleasant social atmosphere to take the place reserved for psychic growth.
17. Psychic science helpfully points out that what ever is wrong with a man's world is exactly the same thing that is wrong with the man himself.
18. Events can destroy all of our beautiful dreams without injuring us one bit.
19. If you know you have a confused and divided mind, that is good knowledge, not a reason for despair, for this awareness is the first necessary step to wholeness.
20. Each time you feel you have gone as far as possible, take one more short step.

THE MAN WHO SOUGHT HIS FORTUNE

A young Englishman in the days of knights and

castles was wandering the land in search of his fortune. As he paused to rest by the roadside, a wealthy duke galloped up to question him. Discovering that the young man was skilled in archery, the duke invited him, "Come teach your skills to the men of my castle. As long as I have your loyal service, you can borrow freely of whatever you need from my castle and land. But if you leave, you must go as empty as you came."

Accepting, the young man carried out his duties faithfully. But as the weeks went by he felt restless and unhappy. He could give no reason for his dissatisfaction, for the duke had kept his word in supplying his needs. Then, in a flash of insight, he saw it. When informing the duke that he was leaving, the nobleman asked him why. The young man replied, "Because I have nothing of my own."

How to own yourself

You are now adventuring toward finding and living with what is truly your own. That alone delivers abiding inner satisfaction.

How do we find our own? By first discovering and discarding what does not really belong to our essential nature. Disturbance does not belong to our true nature, so to see how easily we are disturbed by exterior events is a good start toward ending disturbance. This kind of self-awareness produces unique power. With it you begin to see the difference in disturbance being real as an experience but not real as a necessity.

During a class discussion, Donald T. asked, "What causes all those major and minor shocks in our daily contacts with life? A typical case is when a friend suddenly loses interest in our company."

Donald and the class were told, "Why does something shock you? Because you did not expect it to happen. Why did you not expect it to happen? Because you believe people and events should behave according to your beliefs. Why do you have such beliefs? Because they appear to confirm your illusory ideas about yourself. Why do you have wrong ideas about yourself? Because you glued together all your past experiences and called this bundle your individual self. Why do you not drop this illusory bundle? Because you fear that without it you will not know who you are. What would happen if you dropped it? You would have freedom from all shocks."

You have something of your own when you live without inner or outer labels. Society makes man a machine by giving him flattering labels, but truth makes him an individual by taking away his labels. The label-free man is a free man indeed.

One feature of self-freedom is the possession of an amazing boldness. This boldness is far from being the same thing as the insolent aggressiveness of the self-chained person which masquerades as boldness. The liberated individual is bold, yet perfectly calm and undemanding in all situations, for he is not out to prove himself. Having won the supreme battle for self-wholeness, he has nothing to win or lose in the exterior world. He wins every time by casually dwelling above the frantic winning and losing of most men. He comes and goes as he pleases, unattached, yet truly compassionate, aware of everything and afraid of nothing.

A traveler who lost all his possessions in a hurricane was forced to find shelter in a home not his own and to wear poorly fitting clothing not his own. His discomfort impelled him to get back on his own feet as swiftly as possible. This illustrates why people feel so vaguely uncomfortable in daily life. They live with attitudes and social positions and personality traits entirely foreign to their true nature. Their psychic discomfort should make them eager to get back to their original nature as fast as possible.

Don't let the social atmosphere creep into you; make your own atmosphere. Don't let others own you; own your own self. You can do whatever you like with your own property, which is why you should become your own man.

ZENO OF CYPRUS

Zeno, one of the renowned teachers of Stoicism, was born on the island of Cyprus in 336 B.C. When his father, a traveling merchant, visited Athens, he brought back books by Socrates. Read eagerly by young Zeno, their teachings set the course of his life. Though becoming a merchant himself, he had no heart for the world of business. When hearing of the loss of one of his ships, he abandoned commerce for the life of a philosopher. He studied under Crates, who was himself a pupil of the famous Diogenes.

Zeno's fame spread as he taught:

"Natural laws, not man-made laws, are the correct foundation for a happy life."

"Do not be hasty in conclusions, but patiently examine whether an idea is truly right, or whether it is wrongness masquerading as right."

"Valuable knowledge for self-harmony is available to every sincere seeker who pursues it diligently."

Cleanthes, a pupil at Zeno's school, studied his teacher's private life carefully. Cleanthes discovered that here was that rare individual who personally lived the virtues he urged upon others.

Facts about an authentic teacher

An authentic teacher instructs in ways which often puzzle the new student. The baffled student cannot as yet see how he must be gently switched over from mental curiosity to spiritual quest. The pupil might ask, "What rewards can we expect from our studies?" The teacher's reply is designed to cut away the pupil's false assumption that the question was a right one: "Please give attention to self-study alone, otherwise you will unconsciously seek false rewards." This produces a mild shock, which when welcomed by the student, increases his mental light.

"Many of you ramble when you should concentrate," a teacher told his class. "To correct this, I wish each of you to express a good and basic principle in just two words." The class produced: *1. Love truth. 2. Detach yesterday. 3. Reject pretense. 4. Observe feelings. 5. Value maturity. 6. Study conflict. 7. Travel lightly. 8. Release yourself. 9. Abandon idols. 10. Remain enthusiastic. 11. Begin anew.*

For many reasons, it is not easy to approach an authentic teacher. For one, he will not come down to the level of popular illusion; the seeker must make an effort to rise to the teacher's plane of consciousness. Preliminary effort consists of genuine humility and a willingness to learn. Religious charlatans make public contact easy, which means the seeker brings nothing right and can therefore receive no additional rightness. Knowing all this, a true teacher says, "Earn the right to receive and you will surely receive."

A student asked, "I have heard that an authentic teacher has unusual powers of observation. Will you please comment?" Reply: "Yes, a sharp mind makes sharp eyes. His power is natural, but highly developed, because he does not waste his energies in negativities, as do most people. Although he understands people at a glance, he keeps his power quiet. If people knew how easily he reads them, they would be uncomfortable, and therefore less receptive to his teachings."

Deep down, human beings fear that a close association with the truth will end something. Of course it will. It will end man's frantic scrambling for advantage over others, end his painful pretenses, end his unhappiness over a thousand things. The problem is that he identifies himself with everything, including his anxiety. Offer to take away his anxiety and he runs anxiously away. The truth brings an end to man's fear of coming to an end, after which there is no more fear.

Here are six more interesting facts about authentic teachers:

1. All teachers of truth agree on the fundamentals, for example, Christ said the kingdom of heaven was within, while Buddha counseled every man to be his own lamp.
2. When an awakened man speaks, you can feel at the same time an uncompromising power and a spontaneous friendliness.
3. The internal behavior of an awakened man is noncontradictory, and is always consistent with his varying external behavior, but this superior state is unseen by unenlightened human beings.
4. There is no connection between the titles and diplomas and reputations a man may have and his level of spiritual or psychological intelligence.
5. One of the first questions a teacher asks himself when approached by an inquirer is, "How much truth can this person take without getting angry or upset?"
6. You must make your own judgment about the qualifications of any teacher you meet, and to make right judgment you must want self-dawning more than you want a teacher.

WOMAN IN A CRISIS

A young woman was taking a tour of a disreputable section of a foreign city, together with friends from her own country. In the bustle of the crowds she became separated from the others. At first she was amused at finding herself cut off from her friends, but her humor gradually turned to panic. Glancing around in the falling darkness she saw only frightening faces and heard only strange voices. But wishing to think calmly in the crisis, she stood quietly in one place and watched the bustling crowd carefully. Almost instantly she glimpsed the familiar coat of one of the other women of the tourist party, which brought them together. She learned that her friends had also been seeking her.

The pearl of great price

What you want also wants you. If you seek the celestial the celestial also seeks you. There are no unanswered requests in the universe. If we do not like what we are receiving, we can learn to ask for something different. Then, like the woman in the story, we will find what we wish.

To be where we belong in the psychological world provides all the necessary wisdom for supremacy in the everyday world.

Fred G. asked, "May we hear more about acquiring greater wisdom in dealing with other people?" Response: "Your wisdom or non-wisdom in handling others will be exactly the same as your wisdom or non-wisdom in dealing with yourself. It cannot be otherwise. An underground stream will come to the surface according to its own purity or impurity. So we must see the futility of trying to be right with others before being right with ourselves. This is a positive revelation, for it elevates our understanding."

Independent flexibility. That describes your skilled way of handling other people once these ideas become your own. Human relations consist of making contact and declining contact, speech and silence, seriousness and gaiety, but most men never know which one is right for each occasion. You will know every time. Among other insights, you will know at a glance what people want from you, which makes your response a healthy one.

If you observe all of a rug, you understand all its designs, both those in the center and on the edges. But you cannot understand a rug's designs if they are partly covered by furniture; you can only offer risky opinions about them. When you see the whole of life, you also see its parts, but then you do not separate life into parts. Then you can be unwanted, if necessary, because you see that being wanted and being unwanted are parts of the whole life-design. To this new knowledge is added an amazement—the very notions of being wanted or unwanted have no connection with you.

The first time a new truth is touched, its newness is definitely felt, yet at the same time it is brief and uncertain. It is like quickly brushing your fingers against a smooth pearl lost in a bowlful of rough pebbles. But this brief touch is a great moment, for now you can *feel the difference* between rightness and wrongness, which makes the pearl your own.

If we look at a rock on the ground we see it as still, without movement. But a scientist comes along to tell us the rock is hurtling through space, for it is part of the entire earth which hurtles through space. That sudden switch in viewpoints startles us, yet we see how true it is. If we welcome psychic self-startling, we attain the broader viewpoints about ourselves. Here is one of them: You are totally free at the very instant you read this line.

Remember, you are reversing everything—your viewpoints toward yourself and toward your relationships with life. You are reversing the way you think and feel and act. For example, you know how many people waste energy in self-condemnation. What is the reverse of that? Whoever says to himself quietly, "I will direct my strength toward self-understanding" is placing himself on his own side. Reverse something today.

REMEMBER THESE PRINCIPAL POINTS

1. Realize the richness of individual self-search.
2. Tension disappears as we end the false sense of self.
3. To live with truth is to live with new charm.
4. Study with others, but apply these facts personally.

5. Each day take one more short step forward.
6. Own your own self, live your own life.
7. Self-liberty supplies a new kind of boldness.
8. All authentic teachers agree on the fundamental facts.
9. Our right requests attract right responses.
10. Reverse your viewpoints to make them serve your life.

3

How to Make Problems Disappear Forever

THE BUSY MEN

At one time in a California city a site for a new office building was being prepared. Sprawled over the construction area were tall stacks of steel, cement and other building materials. Growling trucks and tractors passed each other in their hauling and pushing. Crews of workmen busied themselves with their various projects on the grounds, while foremen shouted commands. The noisy activities continued over the days.

But a careful observer would have noticed

something wrong. While the activities went on with persistent zeal, the building itself did not rise one foot into the air. In spite of all the movements and changes and commands, the proposed building did not turn into a building at all.

Those who wondered at the activity-without-construction finally heard the answer. A set of plans essential to the upward construction had been lost. When located, the building began to rise.

You are in a good position

This story illustrates man's illusory way: he engages in social activities having no real constructiveness. But he never realizes this because he mistakes mechanical activity for creativity. From this fundamental error comes all his problems.

The individual who sees this for himself has reason to rejoice. He can now replace mechanical movement with conscious creativity. Upon that firm foundation he will rise to self-newness.

Anyone can locate the missing plans which guide his upward construction. He will then surely rise above his problems—the problems which still haunt the busy but unknowing men on the ground level. The following paragraphs contribute to this construction.

Randolph J. came to tell of problems in his home. The marriage had started out nicely enough, but had turned into a series of quarrels and hurt feelings. He said he had tried to change his wife, but nothing changed. Randolph commented, "You say we cannot solve a problem because we do not see the problem. How does this apply to my situation?" Reply: "If you have a difficulty with another person, what good does it do to try to change the other person? You have the problem. You must change." Randolph wisely said he would concentrate on that idea for the next few days.

If we place a difficulty outside of ourselves we will also place its solution outside of ourselves, which creates an absurd and unsolvable situation. Many people claim to see this as a fact, but if difficulties continue, deeper insight is needed. So you are working on yourself correctly when sighting inner conflicts you never saw before. Your daily ways begin to feel strange, like old clothes which no longer fit comfortably. This strange feeling is an essential first step out of the shaky dream-world to the new reality which does not wobble.

State your problem clearly and frankly to yourself. In simple language, lay it out before your mental eyes. Say, "I am terrified at the madness of human society," or "I am depressed over my inability to uplift myself." Do not tell others, but tell yourself about your problem. *Do not try to do anything with the problem, but simply become deeply conscious of it.* A conscious man or woman knows exactly what to do with every problem.

"What is the right thing to do?" remains an unanswered question with most people. It is no problem at all to the man or woman whose diligence has awakened his or her psychic nature. Such a person knows what is right every second, and knows it without a strained thought: anything done or left undone which does not cause inner contradiction is right.

All problems are merely contradictions. All contradictions are caused by the wrong thinking of the conditioned mind which splits everything into opposites—the opposites of friend and enemy, you and I, yesterday and tomorrow and so on. When self-knowledge dissolves this opposite-thinking, this contradictory thinking, all problems disappear. You then see that the problem was not a treacherous friend or a denied desire or a stubborn habit, but only wrong thinking itself.

If we say, "There is a vastness to life which is unseen at present," we are stating a fact. It may not be our experience as yet, but it is still a fact which nothing can destroy. So we are in a good position. From this position we can begin to see life in a different way, the way of non-division, of wholeness. We can begin seeing the entire ocean instead of individual waves. What are some of these waves? Obsessive ambition. Finding false comfort in crowds. Demanding respect. Pretending to know. Individual waves cannot support a ship. But the smooth and entire ocean easily does so.

THE SECRET OF SIR JOSHUA REYNOLDS

Sir Joshua Reynolds, the famous English portrait painter, had a special secret which contributed to his success. It enabled him to produce masterpieces such as "Mrs. Siddons as the Tragic Muse." The secret was simple but extremely practical. Reynolds made a deep and persistent study of the great masters of the past. For example, he traveled to Rome, Genoa and Florence, to study the works of Michelangelo and Raphael. No detail was overlooked, no question remained unanswered. Coloring and style, shading and brushing, all fell under his mental microscope. Upon discovering a new idea or a superior technique, Reynolds applied them to his own paintings. By this procedure he turned the skills of others into his own skills.

The laws of psychic levels

Just as artistic skills are won by persistent men, so are psychic skills gained by those who seek until they find. The knowledge necessary for self-elevation is available to all who want it. For example, every man occupies a particular level of psychological understanding or misunderstanding. A thousand questions a man asks about his life would be answered by his insight into the laws about psychic levels. Also, he would know how to attract only beneficial people and events. Knowledge of the following principles will draw these benefits to you:

1. A man's psychic level, high or low, determines the kind of life he leads, for either happiness or frustration.
2. Every man unconsciously chooses his own level, which means a wise man will try to see his own responsibility for the kind of life he experiences.

3. An individual automatically seeks out others on his own level, for like attracts like.
4. All attempts by a man to behave on a higher level of goodness or intelligence or relaxation than that supplied by his present level will fail, producing self-contradiction and depression.
5. The sure way to stop getting hurt and exploited by others is to put distance between your plane and theirs.
6. A man never believes that he occupied a certain low level of misunderstanding until he rises above it and sees the difference for himself, which is why it is difficult to talk to people about their need for transcending themselves.
7. Knowledge alone does not raise a person's level, but when knowledge combines with the surrender of psychic stubbornness, inner uplifting is certain.
8. Anyone who is weary enough of his present level can start to raise himself by using esoteric techniques.

We must not take a cosmic principle as some outside authority which seeks to impose its will on us. An unclear mind makes this mistake, even thinking that the principle threatens its happiness. *What* happiness? There is no you *and* a cosmic principle which seeks to impose itself upon you, for at the very moment you hold this book you are the principle itself. As this is realized, your own light shines through. You become yourself!

People are puzzled when told they must not merely

think about the truth but must actually become the truth. Mental clarity will come as they realize that God, Truth, Reality is the only power, that nothing is apart from Reality. Since we are not separate from Reality, there is not Reality *and* us; there is only one item and we are included in that oneness. In this state of non-division a man possesses the truth, but the truth also possesses the man. This kind of man is fearless.

Arthur B. said he was fascinated by these ideas but admitted he was not sure what it meant to work with them. He became clear as he heard, "To work with higher ideas means to connect them with your daily experiences. For instance, where has your attention been for the last twenty-four hours? On how badly people treat you, or on observing the ways of your own mind? On a frantic attempt to feel secure, or on a program for shattering harmful responses to daily challenges? On listening to the noise of an ailing world, or on ways to live from your purified nature?"

Since positive awareness and negative thought cannot occupy the same space in your mind, you can make room for whichever one you prefer.

WHY THINGS HAPPEN AS THEY DO

One teacher of higher truth was famous for his short and pointed answers to questions from his students. During one teaching session a student commented, "We wish to know why our lives unfold the way they do. Why do we experience our happinesses and sorrows, our successes and failures?"

Replied their teacher, "For the next seven days, observe what happens to you as a result of what you do."

Seven days later the students reported what happened to them as a result of their own actions:

"When my mind wandered I dropped a dish."

"I acted impulsively and two hours later regretted it."

"My thoughts about myself made me nervous."

"I spoke gently to an angry man and he replied gently."

When asked for more of an explanation for the assignment, the teacher supplied one of his short but meaningful answers: "Don't you see? Observe how you unknowingly create your present world, for then you will be able to knowingly create a new world."

Let understanding banish self-concern

How simple the lesson really is:

1. Each person makes his inner day whatever it is.
2. Each person can create a new inner day for himself.

When a man looks into a mirror he sees himself. It would be absurd for him to believe that the eyes and ears and hair are part of the mirror. But a man looks out at the world and thinks it is different from his own projections about it. If this is understood at the very start—that we see ourselves in whatever we see—the process of self-healing begins.

Eric V. possessed an intense interest which widened his view very swiftly. It all started when he asked his first question in class: "What am I doing wrong when I feel menaced by people and events?" Reply: "You still think the enemy is outside. It is not. A tornado tears up a town because it is inside that town, not outside it."

It takes a lot of courage to give up having enemies. Does that sound like a strange thing to say? Listen. Unawakened people demand enemies, for enemies provide a fierce agitation, an emotional thrill, which they tragically think is life, but which is misery. As we dare to give up enemies we enter a void, experience it fully and eventually emerge on the other side to true life.

Everyone has areas calling for special consideration. Some must reflect upon their inability to be friends with themselves, while others must consider how often their emotional floods carry away their natural logic. But everyone should concentrate with maximum force upon this area: think about what it means to be in a state of psychic hypnosis.

The hypnotic belief that man can escape the jungle through mechanical thinking is all a hoax. It is such a gigantic hoax that few see through it. There is a thick wall in man's mind which prevents him from seeing it even when he suffers terribly from his own mechanicalness. You can see through it. You can escape the jungle. You can do it with conscious thought.

When a huge and hazardous iceberg is spotted in the Atlantic Ocean, it is carefully charted and followed by patrol boats. When the iceberg eventually drifts into warm waters, it disappears, leaving the patrol with no more work to do. This is how our inner work leads to a healthy lack of concern for ourselves. By carefully following a worry or a disappointment, we see it drift into the warm waters of our expanded understanding, where it disappears.

This question was asked by a visitor who accompanied a regular student to the class: "Instead of self-study, why can't we just find happiness by losing ourselves in interesting activities?" Answer: "Because when you lose yourself you do just that— you lose yourself in self-division. It is like laughing at a party while knowing you must later walk home alone in the dark. Happiness resides in the here and now, which contains no self-division."

A botanist unexpectedly discovered a rare and beautiful flower growing on the heights of the Alps. But he did not have the equipment needed for carrying the delicate flower down the mountain. Later, when prepared, he had his flower. Be ready! That is the secret of inner achievement. Be ready to place the invisible world before the material world. Be ready with a "Yes" when asked to increase self-study.

THE WEALTHY MERCHANT

A merchant of ancient India owned many bazaars which returned him rich profits every day. He kept his shops supplied with attractive merchandise by making large purchases at seaports and national borders. It was his great delight to search out and purchase low-priced shipments of silk and spices and perfumes.

One day, while visiting one of his bazaars, he was introduced to a man with a reputation for great wisdom. The merchant asked the wise man for advice for obtaining new riches. The wise man replied, "Journey to the mountain range north of here which overlooks the peaceful river. Remain quietly on its highest peak until you see something you never saw before."

Speeding there on his fastest horse, the merchant waited and watched. In imagination he dreamed about vast quantities of profitable merchandise coming his way. But at the end of three days he had seen nothing except the natural beauties of the surrounding lands. In annoyance and confusion, the merchant rode back to the wise man to say, "I obtained no riches. What went wrong?" Replied the wise man, "Your idea of riches."

What esotericism is all about

When having no false values we have no false aims. When having no false aims we do not create the problems and sorrows which follow false aims.

In our early explorations we must remember that esoteric riches are entirely different from what we might imagine. If we imagine them we merely think with old notions which are incapable of discovering the new. We must take care that we do not explore with an eagerness to find merely what we would prefer to find. When we find what is truly right, we are truly right.

Ask yourself, "What if true life is utterly and amazingly different from what I now think it is?" Next, every day consider that it might be so. It is so.

Peggy C. commented, "You say that problems and conflicts have a hypnotic attraction to our minds; that we like to dwell on them. I know this is true because I find myself returning again and again to an unpleasant incident in my past. How can we break this negative habit?"

Peggy was told, "It falls away of itself as you sense true values. Suppose someone hands you a jar containing dozens of pebbles with a dull appearance. You are then told that hidden among those pebbles is a sparkling ruby. Now, where does your attention go? To the ruby. You do not waste your time on pebbles."

Individual problems arise because the sufferer does not understand what is individually wrong. Happily, there is a way to understand what is wrong. It consists of impartial self-observation. This understanding of what is wrong is exactly the same thing as knowing what is right. To see wrongness clearly, directly, deeply, is to know rightness. Awareness that you have taken the wrong fork in the road is also awareness of the right road. Whoever studies wrongness scientifically, while neither evading nor fearing it, will be free of it. If you take the right fork in the road you cannot suffer from the wrong road.

The fact that you are now heading toward a new destination is all that counts. Difficulties and lack of results are as nothing. Anxiety over progress should not occupy your mind for one second. The fact that you are on the right track at last is your supreme victory.

What is esotericism all about?

Instead of anxiously inventing activities in which to conceal a hounding loneliness, would it not be much better to have total freedom from loneliness? Rather than worrying over what will become of us in future years, is it not much superior to completely dissolve a false sense of self with all its worries? Instead of facing another day of frustrated ambitions, would we not prefer to be in quiet Oneness with whatever the day brings? Rather than being tugged back and forth by inner doubt, do we not wish to have a natural wisdom providing effortless guidance?

This is what it is all about.

HOW THE SHIP SUCCEEDED

It was a great day for hundreds of citizens of a Danish coastal village, for a new ship was about to be launched. Constructed with great care by men who enjoyed their work, the ship was designed to sail the seas of the world, delivering and returning rich cargoes. It was not a large ship, but was solid, trim, practical.

At noon on the great day, town officials led the citizens on a happy march to the freshly painted ship. The mayor gave a short speech, then raised his hand as a signal for the ship to slide into the sea. The crowd watched eagerly for the first sign of movement—which failed to come. Once more the mayor signaled for the launching, but again the ship remained in place.

Some workmen investigated. They found that some of the holding blocks had not been removed. When taken away, the ship slid down with a splash, to begin its new life in its natural element.

How to remove mental blocks

A new life in its natural element—that is our destination. So we must locate and remove those blocks which prevent our launching. What are some of these blocks?

1. Timidity toward the new and the unknown.
2. Lack of self-knowledge.
3. Failure to use suffering for self-awakening.
4. Unawareness of the depth of one's actual confusion.
5. Remaining floored by discouragement.
6. The false assumption that one already knows the answers.

7. Preferring temporary thrills to eternal values.
8. Finding false security in popular illusions.
9. Fear of what others may think of one's wish for self-change.
10. Lack of persistence in breaking out.

India's teacher, Sri Ramakrishna, told a story which illustrates several of these blockages, especially points 4 and 7. He tells of a small child who amuses himself by playing with the pigeons in the yard. The child is so absorbed by the pleasure of his play that he fails to notice the absence of his mother. But when tired of playing, when the fun is exhausted, the child suddenly realizes his separation from his mother—and he cries.

We can summarize blockages by saying they are always caused by misunderstandings. A person simply does not see what it is possible for him to see. With a new knowledge, the barriers fall away of themselves, opening him to the vastness of psychic seas.

Study the next two paragraphs for new knowledge regarding human relations.

Never forget that a person is as kindly or unkindly to others as he is to himself. This is unbreakable psychic law. Suppose you see a man who likes to put pressure on others. It is an extension of the same pressure he has first put on himself by misunderstanding life. So what would you tell someone who complains about the constant pressure he feels? Ask him, "Is anyone causing you to suffer at this very moment—or are you suffering because of the way your mind is operating at this very moment?"

Success against the pressures of organized society can be won only by whoever has first achieved psychic self-organization. This success comes not by angrily battling against the various pressures, but by seeing through self-pressures which create the illusion that the pressures are outside. The victorious man formerly had a compulsion to take sides with one pressure group against another pressure group, but now sees his error. He now knows that the mind which takes sides can never know truth and liberty, for these virtues reside above the taking of sides.

Clifford R. commented, "I seem to have blockages in my work and my career. I need to understand the connection between earning my living and the inner adventure. Please say something about these two areas." Reply: "Earn your living in any normal way and forget about it. Place no value on what society calls success, which is nothing but exhausting attempts at self-proving. Give importance only to what you are doing with yourself as a human being here on earth. But use your employment for attaining higher awareness. For example, observe the chaos around you and determine that you are not going to be one of those self-wrecking human beings."

Do not take these ideas as lofty ideals which sound good when preached in public. That is also a blockage. Take them as the life-transforming facts that they are.

THE EXPOSED HOAX

A group of scientists were working on an important project which promised to improve human health. However, their country was at war, which made their work more difficult. One evening, while conducting some vital experiments, the lights began to flicker off and on, and the equipment faltered. Checking the dozens of switches and connections, they found nothing wrong, which left them in confusion. The electricity failed several more times during the following days, but they could not locate the source of the problem.

Finally, special guards investigated the entire building, inside and out. They returned to the scientists with the report, "There is nothing at all wrong with the building or the equipment. It was all a hoax by enemy agents. They managed to control the incoming power lines long enough to cause delay and confusion. But it will not happen again. We have guards at the right places."

Examine these profound principles

The point of this story is powerful. Life's problems are caused by a trick which we fail to see as a trick. Being unaware of the actual cause of our grief—our own psychic hypnosis—we stumble around in the dark, never realizing how different everything could be.

Here is a clue for exposing the trick: when investigation revealed the nature of the trick played upon the scientists, what happened to their problem? It vanished.

Blue skies appear to whoever finally sees how he is making a problem where none really exists. He is hurt when his business enterprise fails? Its success could have added absolutely nothing to his true nature, which is already complete. He is tense because something threatens to disturb his secure ways? His security was never in those ways in the first place, so the problem itself is false. These ideas are for vigorous minds to ponder.

Owen K. raised his hand to say, "You requested us to ask clear and direct questions, which I will do. How can we live untroubled in a troubled world?" Reply: "By seeing that you are just as much the sea as the swimmer in the sea. The sea is stormy only when there is a supposedly separate swimmer who opposes it. The opposition causes the storm. There is truly no battle between the swimmer and the sea, for they are simply two representatives of the same movements of life as a whole. We will review this in future sessions."

Do you see why the theme of self-unity, of Oneness, is so important to understand? It is because Oneness places us on our own side, which delivers lasting happiness. That wise Dutch philosopher, Baruch Spinoza, explained it like this: *"For there is nothing more useful to man than that which most agrees with his own nature."*

Problems Disappear Forever

A person is in psychic health when he is one with himself, when he is his own friend. Perhaps you know people who are separated from themselves by frantic desires, fearful imaginations, sour attitudes, by regrets of the past and demands upon the future.

When hearing of principles such as that of Oneness, people are apt to react, "It is a fascinating study, but how can it help my shaky marriage or end my worries over money or reduce my tension toward the future?"

This question is answered throughout the book, but a summary will help. People have these problems precisely because they do not understand and live within these principles. They take esoteric topics as interesting excursions but not as the authentic answers that they are. You can proceed more wisely. When confronted by any difficulty, connect it at once with the higher facts you have learned. Somewhere among these facts is your solution and your relaxation.

The single great human problem is not war or bad government or poverty, but the psychic sleep of men, which causes all other problems. And there is no difference in sleeping men except in the ways they pretend to be awake.

To be awake is everything.

LET THESE TRUTHS GUIDE YOUR DAY

1. Living in cosmic consciousness solves all problems.
2. Both the problem and the solution are within ourselves.
3. Collect problem-dissolving facts and reflect upon them.
4. As our psychic level rises, our difficulties vanish.
5. Connect cosmic principles with your daily experiences.
6. Enemies are abolished immediately with these truths.
7. By valuing true riches we attract those riches.
8. Natural wisdom handles all challenges perfectly.
9. You are learning how to be your own best friend.
10. Self-awakening is the supreme adventure in life.

4

Secrets for Harmonious Human Relations

THE CROWD IN THE STREET

A father and his son lived in a chaotic country. The father waited for the right opportunity to teach his son to live properly while in troubled times. The opportunity came when a band of bandits attacked and looted their village, then disappeared swiftly. The son wanted to join the enraged crowd in the street, but his father told him, "Stand at the window and look out. See that man with the angry face? Do you want to destroy yourself with anger?"

"No," said the son.

"Observe that man over there who is actually trembling with fear. Do you want to go through life being afraid?"

The son replied, "I do not."

"Notice that man who is running around with frantic jerks of his arms," said the father. "Do you want to be a person with no control over himself?"

"No, I do not want to be out of control," assured the son. The young man sensed that his father was trying to tell him something of supreme importance, but could not quite grasp the complete meaning. The next day he asked, "What was behind your words of yesterday?"

His father told him, "Never let mechanical people tell you how to respond to any kind of event. Respond from you own essence, for that is the only healthy response. Then you will not be a helpless leaf tossed about by every passing wind, which is the way most people live—and suffer. Live only from your true nature."

How to end a thousand difficulties

People panic in a crisis because of a wrong reaction. The main wrong reaction is to think the crisis has an exterior cause, when in fact a personal crisis is a *personal* crisis. The corrective course in any crisis is to react with the thought, "Something is unnecessarily agitating within me." Insight into pointless agitation ends it, for no man consciously agitates himself. In this way you do not find an answer to a crisis; you dissolve the crisis itself.

One cause of guilt and frustration is the inability to tell the difference between man-made laws and spiritual laws, which are often opposed to each other. Self-awareness sweeps out this problem once and for all. The self-illuminated man knows just what to do in every situation involving various laws, for spiritual rightness understands and transcends human wrongness.

Think about the need for right motives. A motive is the seed which determines the quality of the fruit. It is a wonderfully right motive to wish to know right and wrong from your own mind, not from what others tell you is right and wrong. Consider the motives of two kinds of public speakers. An unawakened man speaks to convince himself that his illusions are realities. The enlightened man speaks to show others that their realities are illusions.

Have you ever thought of words as petty dictators which command you to feel dejected or defeated? That is what they are, which means you must no longer let mere words rise up and tell you how to feel. Don't let the word "weakness" arouse feelings of shame; don't let "failure" frighten you. Our emotional responses to words are unconscious, which means we must alertly notice how a word arouses a feeling. Be aware of the mechanical process, for this ends the power of words to whip you about.

Imagine a printing press turning out newspapers having several spelling mistakes in the headlines. Workmen grab the emerging papers and frantically try to make corrections—but no one thinks to correct the single cause of all the mistakes, which is the printing press itself. No printer would make that kind of error, but society does it every day by trying to correct effects instead of causes. Unconsciousness is the faulty printing press; consciousness is the correction.

One flash of insight can clear up a thousand difficulties. Lloyd H., who was faced with domestic difficulties, could see no way out. However, Lloyd knew enough to work at clarifying his own mind. When he changed his attitude toward the difficulties, their power over him disappeared. At a group meeting he stated, "Where is the answer to a problem? I found out. It is above the mind that argues back and forth about it."

Citizenship in the spiritual kingdom liberates us from worldly grief, just as a citizen of a South American country is uninvolved with the problems of a European nation.

AGATHON AND CYRUS

There was once a man named Agathon who understood the secrets of life. He had a neighbor named Cyrus. Whenever they met, Cyrus talked only about topics of interest to himself, such as social affairs and business, but never asked Agathon about anything.

One autumn, Cyrus became involved with a woman, which turned into a disaster for him. The next time he met Agathon, Cyrus snapped accusingly, "You are supposed to have a mind which understands all things. Why did you not warn me about that woman?"

"You did not ask me," replied Agathon.

The following winter, Cyrus invested a considerable sum of money in a fishing enterprise, which collapsed. The bitter Cyrus once more accosted Agathon: "With your knowledge of human events, you could have prevented my loss. Could you not have advised me?"

Inquired Agathon, "Could you not have asked me?"

The next spring, Cyrus was about to engage in several new activities, both social and financial. For an entire week he thought about them, while remembering his past disasters. Finally, he put on his coat, walked over to Agathon's home and said, "Friend Agathon, there is something I would like to ask."

Self-trust is true trust

Cyrus is representative of the hurt and confused person who has reached the end of his rope—and then has the solid sense to let go of his imitation wisdom. Such a person suspects the existence of another way to live, a way which is above his mechanically repeated errors and injuries. Such a person is teachable, and that is everything.

Marie J. came to say she had lost her way in life. Neither her marriage nor her career served as guides any longer. "Not knowing what to do is the main torment," she explained. "I don't know how much longer I can take this endless agitation." Marie heard as a reply, "This may sound too simple to you, but suppose all can be changed by changing the way you think. Will you start with this principle and go on from there?" Marie agreed, which was her right start.

The only difference between scattered stacks of metal and a soaring airplane is what eager minds and hands do with the metal. So be happy when reality scatters your beautiful dream and be doubly happy when you proceed creatively after the scattering. Tell yourself, "There is another way to think toward this condition," for, in fact, there *is* another way, which an eager mind will find.

There is one power which is always and instantly available. No one can ever deprive you of your natural ability to choose a different and richer life for yourself. Nor can events and circumstances take away your right to become a new man or new woman. And this is all that matters. If all else falls apart, this is as steadfast as the universe itself. We need only remember that though we are not as yet fully awake, the truth is.

The only trust is self-trust. Even when you inquire of an authentic teacher it is your own understanding which responds to the knowledge he offers. Someone may ask, "But how can I trust myself when I realize my confusion?" Your realization of confusion is the beginning of genuine self-trust, for you are abandoning false self-trust, which consists of reliance upon illusory strength. A deep realization of self-confusion produces a miracle of insight in which you see that trust in yourself and trust in the truth are one and the same.

You can give yourself everything you need. You can give yourself the ability to respond to a disappointment just as if it did not happen to you at all. You can supply your own needed encouragement for removing a crisis. You can provide self-strength for shaking off the costume of an imitative life and live from your own essence. You are both your own powerhouse and your own electricity.

Aid is everywhere. Want it deeply and you will have it abundantly. The truth has a flood of enthusiasm which wants to reach you just as much as you want to reach it. The use of one aid reveals another aid. Here are aims for immediate use:

1. Use anxiety to end anxiety.
2. Experiment with your absorbed knowledge.
3. Ask questions about your way of life.
4. Try to feel the good in goodness.
5. Be your own inspiration.

MICHELANGELO AND THE STONE

During a class session a pupil said to his teacher, "You say that our true nature knows what to do in every daily situation. I find this difficult to understand. Where am I thinking incorrectly?"

The teacher explained that our true nature does in fact know what to do, so our confusion is a result of not releasing its power to perform its perfect work in daily affairs. "Confusion," the teacher explained, "simply means that we are still inwardly divided. One part of us wants one thing and an opposing part wants another thing, leaving us frustrated and fearful. Your unified nature is never a problem to itself, therefore, it never creates exterior problems in the first place."

The teacher then provided this illustration: "The authorities at Florence requested a sculptor to carve a statue from a huge block of stone which had an awkward shape. The sculptor tried, but soon gave up, declaring that the strange shape of the rock made work impossible. The authorities then asked Michelangelo to work on it. Because Michelangelo was Michelangelo, he carved from the rock his famous statue of David."

The teacher's lesson concluded with, "*Be* and you will *do*."

The true meaning of love

The last five words of this story deserve special consideration. What do they mean? They simply mean we must realize our oneness with life, we must not mistakenly think we are separate from the All. Then, our doing is easy, unopposed, for we do not create opposition by faulty thinking. Then we are just as at ease with what unknowing men call "failure" as with what they call "success," for our undivided mind—our Cosmic Mind—does not live by labels.

When disconnecting ourselves from self-will, to blend with the cosmic flow of life, everything we do is a success—true success.

To understand a truth means to be one with that truth. As long as there is a self *and* the truth there is still separation from that truth. While a truth must first be absorbed by the mental part, it must proceed to be understood by all the other parts which make up the whole man. We must grasp a fact mentally, emotionally, physically, even sexually. This is psychic health, and psychic health means wholeness.

Connect the principle of oneness with the principle of love. In true love there is not love *and* the someone or something which is loved. Such division is the artificial love of a divided mind, which quickly turns to anger when thwarted or rejected. True love is based on self-unity and self-knowledge, also on deep insight into human nature, not on ego-serving sentimentality. Being one with itself, true love is also one with everything in the universe.

So self-knowledge is everything. If you know what you are all about, you know what life is all about. You are not separate from life; you are life itself.

Why does a man persist in false duties and burdensome responsibilities which wear him down? Because he wrongly thinks they are necessary to his psychic survival. If you have a nightmare about drifting down a river toward a waterfall you may fight all over your bed, with tortured nerves. But when awakening you see your right relationship to your surroundings, and so relax. Do you see why self-awakening should be your great aim in life?

Once you really see, it is all so simple. Test it for yourself. How do you feel and how do you act toward someone from whom you want something, perhaps relief from insecurity? In contrast, how do you feel and act toward someone from whom you want nothing? Try to see the great difference. When seeking nothing, you are free, spontaneous, light-hearted. When wanting something, there exists tension, caution, heavy-mindedness. Know that you can have relationships with others without seeking anything from them. That is right relationship.

You can set yourself free by the following method: Whenever you lose something of psychological value, perhaps a person or an object, do not seek a replacement. Live without it until something changes within you, which it will. A refusal to replace an apparent security sets you free.

THE INTELLIGENT SEED

A grateful student returned one day to his former school to bring a gift to his teacher. He happened to arrive just as a new class was about to begin. He took a chair at the back of the hall, but was soon noticed by his teacher. Introducing the advanced student to the class, the teacher told him, "You have learned many things. You must now give your knowledge to others. What do you have to tell us?"

Standing, the student told the following story:

"There is a certain kind of seed with an extraordinary natural intelligence which serves its own true interests. This seed is carried by the wind from area to area, but it never sends out its tiny roots until it reaches friendly and healthy soil. If it finds itself on hard and dry land it remains aloof from the hostile area and rests for a while. Later, when carried by another wind to another place, it tests the new land for suitability. When finding soil which is in harmony with its own nature and its own needs, the roots gladly go out to begin healthy growth."

Twenty invigorating ideas

Like that intelligent seed, we must refuse to settle down in unhealthy human situations. Happily, there is no need for anyone to settle on psychic ground which is foreign to his true nature. We can associate only with whatever is healthy and friendly, such as these thoughts:

1. Where there is right living, there is no concern as to whether that rightness is attractive or acceptable to others.
2. When you find yourself with negative people, separate yourself at once from the psychological atmosphere to remain within the pure atmosphere of your true and free nature.
3. Disappointments would have no chance if we

acknowledged at every encounter how different the other person might be from what we first think he is.

4. Any man can sense that his problem is himself, but the extraordinary man goes beyond that to sense that the solution is also himself.
5. Time has no power to cement your nature, therefore you can now be what you once wanted to be.
6. To say that a man is mistaken but sincere can only lead to great disasters, for authentic sincerity cannot be separated from wisdom and goodness, and those virtues do not make mistakes.
7. One practical talent of consciousness is the way it foresees the consequences of various actions, thus avoiding harmful effects and producing beneficial ones.
8. Fearful people always resist the new and the unknown in psychological matters, so you must not let them delay your progress by listening to their groundless fears.
9. On one side is human belief, which can only divide human beings, while on the other side is consciousness not divided by belief, which alone can unite human beings.
10. A man knows the truth to the degree to which he has no compulsive need to surround himself with others who think as he thinks.
11. We stay out of trouble with others only as we learn to stay out of trouble with ourselves,

for both operate on the same psychological level.

12. A fine first step toward solving any personal difficulty is to realize that you need not remain a question to yourself.
13. If you let others carry a lamp for you, they may lag or rush ahead, but carry your own lamp and it is impossible to ever be out of the light.
14. Your task is to find yourself, which is made easier by realizing that it is not your task to anxiously live up to what others expect of you.
15. There is no way to think correctly without first becoming aware of incorrect thinking, so consciousness of the negative is truly positive.
16. It is only when we begin to think seriously about our negative condition that we can begin to think lightly about it, just as a wanderer feels lighter with each homeward step.
17. If you will thoroughly explain yourself to yourself you will never need to explain yourself to anyone else.
18. Can you see the difference between trying to live and simply living?
19. Rightness never requires agreement from others, only from our true nature, so we must be more interested in being right than in having allies.
20. What we want is the release of our own confined wisdom, just as seeds released to the wind finally take root.

THE ACCUSATION

A man was accused of being tight-fisted toward his wife, of not giving her enough money to run the home properly. He denied the accusation by saying, "But I earn a good salary, so why do you think I would be stingy?"

Replied his accuser, "Several people have commented on how you begrudge her any money for household expenses."

"But I consider myself a generally generous man."

"Why do you continue to defend yourself when everyone knows about your unkindness toward your wife?"

"All right," said the accused man, "I will stop defending myself, but maybe I had better tell you something."

"What?"

"I'm not married."

Do not sacrifice yourself to others

Man is not so well informed about himself as was the individual in the story. Falsely believing he possesses a separate self, an individual identity which must be protected at all costs, man ruins himself and his neighbors in defense of an illusion.

You are "not married" to those life situations which you may think you are. This means you can be free of useless burdens and apologies just as soon as this is realized deeply. It is not your responsibility to be publicly attractive—it is your pleasure to become a clear-minded and mature man or woman. It is not your duty to sacrifice yourself to those who exploit you by trying to make you feel guilty—it is your noble task to see through them.

A man owes nothing to any other human being on earth except to be himself, but since few see this, most men stagger under the burdensome debt of artificial behavior. It is tragic illusion that we can do anything for others before we have done something for ourselves.

"I am bothered," admitted George B., "by feeling that I am not generous enough, that I may be selfish." Response: "Drop the words *generous* and *selfish* completely. They have no meaning except that which confused society gives them; they are chains. Is it generous to help others when the unconscious motive is to expand a flattering self-picture of being a generous person? Is it selfish to refuse to contribute to the jungle performance which society calls a garden party? Don't think from mere words. That opens the door to understanding."

The most generous act you can ever perform for others is to concentrate day and night on your own psychological liberation.

People are worn out by trying to be true to so many things in daily life. Not only is it tiring but also very confusing, for faithfulness to one position brings trouble from another position. If you salute one soldier you are fired upon by another soldier in a different uniform, which is maddening. Spiritual trueness is much simpler, a thousand times easier. If you will be true to this very moment, this eternally new moment, you need do nothing else.

A five-year-old boy can catch a gently tossed ball, a ten-year-old can catch a harder toss, a fifteen-year-old can handle an even harder toss. It is no different in our growing skill in catching and retaining the thoughts we need for self-renewal. The increase in psychological maturity is in itself the increase in skill. So we have nothing to do but tend to our inner development.

A man wrote to a lecturer on truth whom he had heard the day before. His note simply said, "Dear Sir: You *know.*" That man's self-work had given him the ability to recognize a certain amount of truth when he heard it. That entitled him to more truth. Insight into either truth or error in ourselves provides equal insight about truth or error in other people. With this insight we swiftly gather our pearls of truth, for we don't waste time mistaking empty shells for pearls.

When Lewis E. asked for general information on human relations, he was told, "As long as you make no claims on anyone you can enter into any human relationship you like. It is claiming, based on false ideas about security, which causes anxiety and finally heartache. See this for yourself. See that where you have no claims, you easily walk in or out, whichever you please."

SOCRATES AND THE NOBLEMAN

One day Socrates was walking down a street with some friends when a nobleman approached. As was customary, Socrates greeted him, but the nobleman walked straight past, declining to return the courtesy. The friends of the philosopher were angry at the nobleman, but Socrates used the incident to teach a lesson.

"Suppose," said Socrates, "you meet a man on the street with poorer clothing than your own? Would that make you angry? Why then are you angry at a man who has poorer mental habits than you possess?"

The friends of Socrates were enlightened by hearing of this totally new way to respond to a so-called insult.

Let your feelings work for you

Connect a situation in your day with a basic principle you have learned. Are you disturbed by a person with whom you work? All right. Knowledge tells you it is unnecessary to be disturbed by anyone, so examine yourself. Find out why you permit this person to dictate over your emotions, ask why you choose to be disturbed instead of being perceptive. People always want to know how they can do something good for themselves. This is it.

Asked a pupil, "How can we use our feelings as tools for self-release?" Reply: "When drinking water you can feel whether it is cool or hot. A man can also distinguish between cool and comfortable feelings and hot and disturbing feelings. If you feel hot over an insult to your intelligence, be aware of how *your* feelings burn *you*. Next, give up the false pleasure of feeling so indignant, which is self-righteousness anyway."

Hurt feelings play an extremely important role with both self-working and non-working people, but in different ways. To the non-working person, hurt feelings are unconscious and they are resented. Since these states are psychologically unproductive, they keep alive the habit of hurt feelings. The self-working person tries to make hurt feelings conscious, for he knows this will end them. Far from resenting injured feelings, he happily realizes that any negative state can be used for its own destruction.

Just as we must learn to think in a new way, we must learn to listen with originality and freshness. Emerson wisely observed that every man has a right to his own ears. This means we need not listen to either social propaganda or to our own internal distresses as if they are voices of authority. Be aware of them, but reject them as powers. Take these two steps:

1. Ask yourself, "What do I listen to all day long?"
2. Remember that the only true voice is that of your own unified mind.

To have a new life, rebellion is essential, but we must rebel against the right thing. It is useless and frustrating to rebel against unwanted experiences or cruel people or the social system. Such rebellion leaves us on the same psychic level, even if we succeed in changing exterior conditions. We must rebel against our own psychic sleep, which we may already dimly suspect. That changes us magnificently.

Our level of mental maturity determines the value of our involvements in life. From this we see that our own minds are also responsible for the consequences of our involvements, for either shipwreck or smooth seas. The law of cause and effect operates unceasingly here. Examine your consequences. Next, track them back to all your involvements with people and places and events. Next, track back your involvements to the mind which wanted them. What must be changed and uplifted? Do you see how to change involvements and their consequences?

Our major motive must not be to change something in the exterior, but to become conscious of something in the interior, for consciousness alone produces authentic change.

"After some very interesting work on myself," Marlene W. told the class, "I no longer repeat a careless mistake I used to make. Correction started when I noticed how often I found myself in an uncomfortable spot with others. Tracing it back I saw how I brought it on myself by making impulsive promises I later regretted. Because I wanted to be liked I promised to do favors for others, which really made me their servant. Thanks to these teachings I am now a bit wiser. I am living my own life."

Marcus Aurelius wrote, *"To recover your life is*

in your power." That recovery comes more swiftly by letting our human experiences add to our self-insight.

PONDER THESE OUTSTANDING FACTS

1. You can learn to respond perfectly to human events.
2. Learn to correct causes in human events, not effects.
3. Genuine love is founded upon self-wholeness.
4. Self-health naturally creates healthy circumstances.
5. See human nature as it is, not as it appears to be.
6. Explain yourself to yourself, not to others.
7. No person and no circumstance has power to injure you.
8. Your greatest gift to others is an enlightened mind.
9. Your aim is to be true to your original nature.
10. Use all experiences with others for self-insight.

5

Become a New Person with New Conquests

THE SLEEPING BUGLERS

In the early days of South America there existed a primitive tribe which knew nothing about the world surrounding their campground. Frightened at the challenge of exploring unknown territory, they struggled along in their limited ways. But there arose among them a chief of unusual courage and daring. Wishing to provide a better life for his people, the chief took some animal horns and made workable bugles from them. Then he told his people, "We have new worlds to conquer, so let us begin our explorations. Each morning, an hour before sunrise, a bugler will awaken us. Each day we will explore in a new direction from here. We start tomorrow morning."

But next morning, the appointed bugler overslept, so a second bugler was appointed to awaken the first bugler. But the second bugler also overslept, so a third bugler was instructed to awaken the second bugler who would then awaken the first bugler. But the third bugler also failed to awaken in time.

Wishing to turn a human weakness into strength, the chief called his people together once more. "Great wonders await whoever takes a new responsibility for himself," the chief announced. "So from now on, each person will awaken himself. There are ways to do this, which I will show to you. So that you can find something entirely different from the limited region you now inhabit, awaken yourselves every morning. And remember, the exploration itself is energizing."

Eight signs of self-elevation

Expand your inner world by exploring the following paragraphs.

When you are hungry you do not stand around and let others tell you about food. You don't need their descriptions of bread and fruit; you need the food itself. If we are still spiritually hungry it is time to refuse mere descriptions of reality in favor of reality itself. Remember, self-transformation begins the moment we are tired of being what we are, followed by the channeling of our energies toward self-knowledge, not toward battling against so-called exterior enemies.

How can a person stand up for himself in the true meaning of that phrase? By understanding that he does not consist of his acquired sense of self. This must be understood at the start, otherwise everything else he does will be futile and frustrating. A man must see that his basic self is not made up of his memories, his self-pictures and his labels by which he feels himself to be a separate person who must compete with other people. Strangely, we stand up for ourselves by losing what we have called ourselves.

Remarked Elaine S., "I see the need for dropping my wrong ideas about myself, but I feel nervous about doing so." Reply: "Is it frightening to see that you do not exist in the way you assume you do? Of course not. There is not the slightest fright in not being what our illusions insist we are. Try not being the person you believe you are, and see what exists on the other side. There is no fear on the other side."

You need not fear to not know who you are. A lack of labels or identities does not cause fear. It is just the reverse—labels cause fear. Every new label is a new shudder, for it must now be anxiously protected against all that seems to oppose it, all that bears a different label. Since labels are suppressed below the level of awareness, we deny their existence emphatically. Even the loud denial could be a clue for us, but it is also rejected. Reality has no labels. The only answer to "Who are you?" is total silence.

Perhaps you have noticed the prominent position in this book of words such as "dissolve" and "disappear". These words help to convey a major principle of self-transformation. Our first task is not to make anything appear, but to make something disappear. Through conscious work we want to make misleading imaginations and attitudes vanish. Disappearance must come before appearance. Disappearance makes possible the appearance. Let your old coat disappear from your back and you are ready for a new one. Study with this in mind.

When does something become important to you? Why, when you connect it with your own benefit. We see the importance of taking a vacation or reading a book when seeing how they can provide health or happiness or relaxation. Let yourself see the personal importance of cosmic facts. Your permission is all they need in order for them to provide what you need.

Here are eight signs that one is on the right track at last:

1. A deep wish for self-transformation.
2. Intense self-honesty.
3. A willingness to study one's actual state.
4. Increasing awareness of something being wrong within.
5. Distaste for the old and mechanical ways of living.

6. Rejection of false advice and shallow codes.
7. Increasing ability to stand all alone.
8. A sensing of a totally new way to live.

WHEN THE DANCING ENDED

There was once a traveling businessman who was very unhappy with his life. One afternoon while traveling along the rim of a canyon, he heard happy voices coming from the other side of the canyon. Glancing over, he saw a group of people in colorful dress who were happily dancing to exciting music. Wishing to join them, he tried to cross a bridge over the canyon, but was stopped by armed guards. Trying other bridges, he was halted each time.

The businessman was furious at being kept away from the dancing people. Though smiling when doing business, he was secretly bitter, not only at the hostile guards but at everyone else.

On one occasion, while anxiously wondering how to get across, he noticed something on the other side. The dancers had stopped dancing for a moment, and the musicians had set down their instruments. And the happy faces had vanished, instead, everyone seemed tired and depressed. The truth struck him. It had all been an outdoor theatrical performance. He had been watching skillful actors and actresses playing the roles of happy people.

With this realization, he felt a strange relief. He no longer felt envious of the dancers nor hostile toward the guards. No longer wishing to cross the canyon, his frustration had vanished. A deep contentment was now his, for he knew he could be happy just where he was. And he was.

Let your viewpoints change

The purpose of the stories in this book is to illustrate and teach fundamental facts about human life. This particular story has many interesting lessons.

One curious feature of mental advancement is how we lose interest in certain answers because we outgrow the questions. The businessman in the story was nagged by dozens of questions, such as, "How can I trick the guard into letting me cross?" and "Why does life cruelly deny me an opportunity for happiness?" His perception into things as they are became a magician's wand which made his tormenting questions vanish. Any traveler on the cosmic trail will never go wrong by meeting everything with the thought, "Things are not what they seem." The second we see illusion *as* illusion is the same second we see fact as fact, and by the fact we are saved.

Truth reveals itself openly, not to cause human suffering, but to make human beings conscious of the suffering they secretly endure, for this exposure is necessary to the cure.

When the class asked for a discussion of discontent, it heard, "Have you ever studied the nature of discontent? Do so. Discontent is one kind of psychic hypnosis which you need not tolerate for one minute. Discontent indicates you have wrongly divided yourself into a seeker who must find something in order to be whole. You are already whole, but do not see what this means. Why do you put up with discontent instead of banishing it through self-understanding?"

We must understand with the feelings as well as with the mind. Mental rightness invites emotional rightness, which enters eagerly, and you then *feel* what you *know*. At the dawning of day, you have only the sun's light, but you soon feel its warmth, also.

If you are on a nature hike and sight a distant grove of trees, you might assume they are oaks with green leaves. But upon closer view they turn out to be sycamore trees with yellow leaves. You do not object to a correction of your first impression, for you are interested in seeing them as they are, whatever they are. That is the intelligent attitude of anyone who wants his life to get off the ground. He will constantly come closer to the spiritual scene, letting corrections make themselves.

Nelson V. commented during class, "You have said that self-awakening changes the way we see other people. May we have a specific instance of this?" Answer: "If we want to remain asleep, the man who tells us the truth about ourselves is our worst enemy, but if we want to awaken, he is our best friend."

THE VISITOR WHO WAS TOO PROSPEROUS

A teacher of esoteric wisdom often held classes outdoors. He stood on a grassy slope, while his pupils sat on blankets below him. From time to time, visitors who had heard of his practical wisdom attended the lectures. On one occasion, a visitor appeared who was quite conspicuous in his expensive clothing and with his flashing diamond ring. During the question and answer period, the visitor stood up and began to talk. However, instead of asking a question he told about all the books he had read and mentioned his many travels in search of the answers to life. He managed to drop in several bits of information about his financial successes and his prominent place in social affairs. When he finally finished, the teacher briefly acknowledged the statements and the session continued.

Later, in a private discussion, the pupils asked their teacher about the talkative visitor. One student asserted, "I would have rebuked him on the spot. He used the class to boast about himself. He needed a lesson or two."

Explained the teacher, "It would have done no good. He is a perfect example of a person who stands in his own way but cannot see it. Do you see his problem? He is too prosperous at the present time; he has identified with money and popularity. He is drifting in dreamy ignorance, never once suspecting it. Perhaps a future loss or tragedy will shock him out of his false happiness. Then, perhaps, he will be receptive to something higher than himself."

Be guided by these profound facts

Do you see how many things this story explains? Now you know why that person who appears so wise and confident in public is secretly miserable. You understand how his self-centeredness keeps him in a psychic prison. You realize how he could use his daily shocks to attain self-liberty.

Psychic shock consists of the difference between reality and illusion, between the conscious and the unconscious. The man who lives totally from reality is shockless. He will observe a shocking human condition, such as war, but will experience no inner shock, for he has cleared his own mind of unconscious war. He is the true man who can help those who really want help. In the words of author Lew Wallace, *"This man has a story to tell."*

It would be helpful to place ourselves in the mind of an awakened man to see how he views a sufferer who comes to him. The sufferer complains he has been betrayed by others, that no one helps him, that hopes turn to defeats and so on. The teacher clearly understands how the sufferer really suffers from himself, from what Eastern wisdom calls *maya*, illusion. But he also knows that the inquirer will reject this, for the end of illusion means the end of the suffering which he secretly cherishes. When the teacher succeeds in proving the advantage of peace over pain, the man matures.

A shepherd was once hypnotized into thinking that he was a great king, and that his sheep were loyal subjects. So the shepherd's every act expressed his delusion, for example, he commanded the sheep to polish his crown and to bring him a royal dinner. The point is, we must recognize the nonsense of a certain idea at the start, otherwise we will not notice the equal nonsense of all else which follows. So a grasp of fundamentals is essential, including this one: The false sense of self can do nothing but create chaos.

That wise book from the East, the *Tao Te Ching*, comes right to the point about false human notions: "Get rid of what you call wisdom and wisdom will appear. Banish your notions about love and justice and those virtues will arise of themselves." As we clear our minds of fixed ideas, we begin to see what this means—and we begin to live those virtues which formerly were only words.

We cannot see a virtue without possessing that virtue, for the seeing and the having are one and the same. Seeing is consciousness and consciousness is virtue. However, if a person deceives himself into thinking he sees and understands a virtue, such as love, he also deceives himself into believing he possesses the virtue. Honest observation of his inner state will reveal whether he truly possesses a particular virtue or not. If he possesses love, will he wish to deceive others?

THE DICTATOR AND THE WINDMILLS

During the twelfth century, a portion of northern Europe was invaded by a tyrannical militarist. He commanded the farmers of the region to double their production of grain, for he needed the profits for protecting his conquest. Also, he ordered the farmers to erect dozens of new windmills for grinding the expected extra grain. Frightened by the cruel practices of the general, the farmers labored long and hard to obey his orders. The general was pleased at the sight of so many new windmills with their revolving sails.

But as the months passed, the general was surprised to find that grain production was no greater than before. In an attempt to solve the mystery, he rode through the farmlands in close inspection. Each time he looked inside one of the new windmills, his surprise turned to shock. While the windmills were turning, they were doing absolutely nothing down in the work areas, which were empty of grain. Not an ounce of extra grain was being produced. Realizing it meant the end of his power, the dictator fled the land.

One of the liberated farmers explained, "Of course it drained our time and energy to build those windmills, but we were too scared to do otherwise. We knew we would have no extra grain for them, but felt that our safety depended upon following orders. The nightmare is over—thank heaven."

How to end false responsibilities

Perhaps you see in this story a parallel with human life. Living in deep and unconscious fear, people labor through their days with useless and tiring tasks. To all appearances they seem to be purposeful, productive, even jubilant, but flashing changes in facial expression tell a story of emptiness, of sullen submission.

They do not see their submission as a completely false responsibility. They do not know they owe nothing to their own dictating negativities. They can begin to throw off the chains by recognizing them as chains, by not carelessly labeling them as duties or excitements or loyalties or responsibilities. It is easier at the start to recognize these tyrannies when seeing them in others. Notice the man who frantically protects his false assumptions. Watch the woman who loves to pounce on another's weaknesses. Be aware of the crowd taken over by violent emotions.

Said Lowell J., "I see the wisdom of becoming aware of negative feelings, such as discouragement, but now seeing it, what next?" Reply: "You would not know you are discouraged if you did not listen to mental phonograph records which tell you that you are. Don't listen to these mechanical tyrants of the past. The present moment is free, and you are in that moment every moment. Insist upon that fact. Let it answer feelings of discouragement."

If you call a dog from across a field the dog will race naturally and directly over to you without wasting time or energy. But through a system of rewards and punishments, the dog can be trained to zigzag pointlessly, thus wasting his natural efficiency. Awareness of our own wrong training, our conditioning, is an essential stage in remaking ourselves. Esoteric education differs from ordinary schooling in that we seek to *unlearn* all the errors and nonsense society has imposed upon us from birth.

The next two paragraphs will contribute richly to your unlearning.

We are rewarded by being what we are and penalized by being what we are. There are no other rewards or penalties. A person whose nature sets another free will be repaid by that very nature. Whoever secretly enjoys another's misery must view that misery from the same dungeon occupied by the other.

Also, time does not exist in either reward or punishment. A good action is instantaneously rewarded; the good action *is* the reward. The instant gentleness is extended toward another person is the same instant you feel that gentleness. The enjoyment of your guest at the dinner table occupies the same time zone as your own enjoyment.

Declare to yourself, "I take full responsibility for my own psychological health." Then, your increasing insight will finally end all useless and burdensome responsibilities toward life in general and people in particular.

THE OUTCASTS WHO CAME BACK

For many years a Bavarian king had been opposed by a group of political agitators who wanted to take over the country for their own selfish purposes. The king was a kindly man who did not wish to punish the offenders, but also would not tolerate their violent schemes. So instead of imprisoning the agitators, the king banished them from the country.

Later, hoping that the outcasts had learned a lesson from their banishment, the king proclaimed a pardon. All the wanderers were invited to return to the land of their birth. As a public symbol of pardon, a lighted lantern was set on top of the palace steps, where it glowed day and night.

Burdened with guilt and anxiety, many of the outcasts refused to return to see the lantern for themselves. They could not believe the good news. But those who came back, the hardy ones, received instant and full pardon.

Return to yourself today

This story should not be taken as sentimentality, but as the practical lesson it is. Your study of these principles is ending that feeling of terror which confronts man wherever he turns—the feeling of isolation. This feeling is nothing but a hoax which you need no longer endure.

No matter how fearfully lost you may feel yourself to be, you need not remain in this feeling. Do not be afraid of feeling like an outcast. This dreadful emotion invades people simply because there are things which are not as yet understood. Keep in mind that the most profitable time to apply these principles is when you feel it is the most hopeless or difficult to do so. Nothing scatters darkness so quickly as sudden surprise by light.

Consciousness is like a magic lamp carried down into a deep and dark dungeon. It has power to dissolve the dragons down there simply by shining on them.

Remember a few things. Remember you are not required to remain the person who may now be making you quite unhappy. Remember your ability to do as an individual what humanity cannot do as crowds and organizations—the ability to become a new person. Remember that your inner work is definitely lifting that feeling of heaviness which may be so difficult to understand at the present time. Remember that your outer life can be what others think is a failure, while your inner life can be what you know is a success.

This will build an enthusiasm having nothing to do with earning more money or with attempting to influence people for self-benefit. This enthusiasm is like a mountain stream which is unconcerned with its surroundings, which wishes only to fulfill its natural function, which is to flow freely. This new kind of enthusiasm does not arise in those who are enthusiastic in public only, but comes only to the individual who is tired of visible enthusiasm.

Out of his tiredness arises the real, and the real is his lasting enthusiasm.

Diane T., a homemaker, said during a class, "We pretend about everything. Everyone is an actor or an actress. How can we return to being real people?" Answer: "If you attend a masquerade party with an uncomfortable costume, you take it off at first opportunity. Become aware of the discomfort of false personality and it will fall off quickly. So come back to your original self."

The man who succeeds in his inner exploration is the man who comes back. He comes back to more of the lessons he must learn. He returns in spite of discouragement or in spite of hearing blunt facts about himself. Some people do not come back. They go away sorrowfully or critically, therefore losing what could have saved them. We must be different. We must come back, a thousand times if necessary, until we reach the harbor we sense is beyond the fog.

Here are accurate guideposts for the journey back home:

1. Observe other people to see how their minds attract their circumstances, then apply this insight to your own affairs.
2. It takes a lot of courage and intelligence to stop trying to save mankind and to start saving ourselves.
3. If you get lost along the path, you can always return, for the path itself can never get lost.
4. The only possible way a human being can attain

his authentic rights is to be a right person within himself.

5. From that first magic moment when a man lets himself recognize higher truth when be meets it, his life is never the same.

THE SECRET PATH

In the days of the early West, the report went out that there was a fabulous source of gold to be found not too many miles from a certain town. Five interested prospectors agreed to join forces in finding the treasure. Each would search one section of the indicated mountains, and if anyone found the gold, all would share equally in it. One of the men finally returned to town with the exciting news that he had found the gold among some heavily-wooded hills. The prospectors then devised a plan for keeping their secret. The original discoverer of the source would mark the way through the woods with secret signs, such as broken twigs and stones set upon leaves. One by one, the men would set out from town and follow the secret path through the woods.

The plan worked perfectly. Because every man was able to recognize the secret signs, all of them reached the gold.

Release your self-light

Those twigs and stones were in plain view of anyone else from town, but would have appeared ordinary, of no value. Those who did not know the secret could *look* but not *see*. This is what happens to many who are exposed to the esoteric secrets which could lead to spiritual gold.

We can learn to recognize the secret signs when we meet them. Have you ever noticed the weariness resulting from your present pursuit of happiness? This is a helpful sign of being on the wrong path. Have you ever wished that you could live without having to explain yourself to anyone? That is a sign that such liberty can be won.

Somehow, we always sense the truth. Anger and despair prove this, for they insist that *our way* must come before the *true way.* So we refuse the good we dimly recognize. The task of an awakened man is to teach the supreme value of fact over fantasy. One teaching procedure is to say to bewildered mankind, "Behind all your exterior pretenses, you know your aching emptiness. Are your cherished delusions worth it?"

"You urge us to permit ourselves to grow," stated Leo C. "Please provide an example." Response: "If we mistakenly credit ourselves with right thinking, we will also wrongly credit others, just as a brush with red paint colors everything else red. This is why people have trouble with people. Men and women always mistakenly assume they live in a world which knows what it is doing. The person who permits this illusion to be seen *as* an illusion removes its destructiveness from his life."

Learn about the tyranny of familiar-but-wrong thoughts. Association with the familiar-but-wrong is like walking near a deep pit covered over with favorite roses. Such thoughts can be recognized and refused by an alert mind. Does the thought require tense defense? It is wrong. Does the thought dream about a more exciting future? It is a pit. Truthful thoughts require no defense nor hope from the future, for they are sufficient in themselves.

If a man realized that he dwells wherever his mind is located, whether in dark jungles or pure sunlight, would that make him more careful about his mental environment?

A spiritual teacher entered the hall and told his waiting pupils, "It is cosmic law that you cannot possess anything you cease to love. This law has great power for you. What do you want to banish? Sorrow? Cease to attach certain self-centered values to sorrow and it will end. Weakness? Stop using weakness as an excuse for irresponsibility and weakness will be replaced by strength." With this, this teacher left the hall.

Only your own enlightened nature knows what is right and best for you. This is why your entire life must revolve around the release of self-light. That light is there and it is there right now. To whom does this light appear? It is really very simple. It appears to whoever refuses to think today the same way he thought yesterday.

When you experience an unpleasant event, do not react in the usual way, perhaps with strong emotions or by blaming yourself or others. Instead, think of it as being out of place in your life. Try to see that it simply does not belong there, any more than a blundering bear belongs in a flower garden. The unpleasant event had a cause, and this new way of thinking reveals that cause, which prevents its repetition.

When you are one with yourself, you control exterior events perfectly, but in the new cosmic way—by not being apart from them, just as you are no longer apart from yourself. Ponder!

HOW AUTHENTIC SELF-NEWNESS APPEARS

1. Have a persistent wish for self-transformation.
2. You can outgrow any baffling problems in your day.
3. Use self-shocks wisely—as lessons in self-liberty.
4. Learn to detect and drop false responsibilities.
5. Let inner wisdom reject invasions of discouragement.
6. Take full responsibility for developing wholeness.
7. Return constantly to what you can do for yourself.
8. You are never required to remain as you are.
9. Your own true nature knows what is best for you.
10. Ponder carefully all these healing principles.

6

How You Can End Pain and Anxiety

THE ARCHER

On a prominent hill near the ancient city of Troy there stood the statue of an archer. The archer held a bow and arrow in his hands, as if ready to shoot. Legend said that the arrow pointed in the direction of a buried chest which contained great knowledge. The chest, according to legend, contained scrolls and letters which revealed the answers to man's life upon earth.

Over the years many men tried to follow the course indicated by the pointing arrow, but failed to find the treasure of wisdom. But one year a man with a daring mind came to study the situation. The first thing he realized quite clearly was that all the old methods for solving the mystery were quite useless. He therefore determined to think in a new way toward the problem. In this fresh state of mind he noticed something unusual. Each afternoon at 3 o'clock the shadow of the arrow pointed between two distant mountain peaks. At the base of those peaks he found the treasure of knowledge he wanted so zealously. From that day on, every man who made an earnest attempt to think in a new way toward the problem always found the wisdom he wanted.

The cause and cure of human suffering

The following paragraphs will enable you to think in an entirely new way about yourself and your life.

Mental dawning occurs when you understand the meaning of the word "identification." To identify means to wrongly take something—anything at all—as being part of what you call your "self." It means to wrongly believe that you have an identity made up of your acquired opinions and hopes, of your various successes and failures. You might wrongly identify yourself as being "a happily married person," or "a person with an exciting life," or as someone who "deserves" appreciation and comfort and security. Identification is no different from a man who would place a sign across his chest reading, "I am wise" or "I am daring."

Now, can you begin to see what causes human suffering? Suffering occurs when other people and daily events refuse to believe these signs, when the signs are ignored or criticized. Who, then, causes an individual's anguish? Not other people, nor changing circumstances, but the individual himself who insists that these self-labels are realities. A complete absence of self-labels gives reality nothing to strike, therefore suffering becomes impossible.

When this was explained to David G., he responded, "I'm sorry, but I don't understand. Will you please go over it again?"

"Let's approach it differently. Suppose you have labeled yourself as being an important person of some kind. This label will always include the demand that others recognize and honor your so-called self-importance. Woe unto anyone who fails to honor your greatness! But since this label is nothing but vanity and imagination—regardless of how many honors you actually receive from society—it will be constantly challenged by reality. This keeps you nervous and hostile, for whenever your assumed importance is challenged you will feel it as a loss to what you call yourself, which is merely a bundle of illusions. This feeling of losing what you label as your self is the basic cause of all human neurosis, sorrow, war, crime, cruelty and every other misery on earth."

David remarked, "Then identification is the same as living from illusions about oneself. And non-identification is the only answer to human conflict and suffering."

"Do you see why? If you do not invest a feeling of self in other people and in exterior conditions, then natural changes cannot produce a painful feeling of loss of self. In this free state you live in perfect serenity, regardless of changes. Suppose a man had to protect a necklace from vicious thieves. It keeps him nervous, tense; he sees enemies wherever he goes. But he discovers that the necklace is a worthless imitation. Seeing that its value existed only in his false beliefs, his worries vanish forever."

David was helped, as you can be helped, by taking these steps:

1. Study and understand the meaning of identification.
2. Never identify with anything.

ABOVE BOTH SIDES

There was once a community of people who lived on one side of a river. They called themselves the Good People, while referring to the residents on the other side of the river as the Bad People. But these residents of the other side called themselves the Nice People, while labeling the others as the Evil People.

One day an outsider traveled up the river. Because he was lonely, he wanted to find a secure home for himself. When asking the self-called Good People about it, they urged him to join their community, while warning against the treachery of the Bad People. But when crossing the river, the outsider heard the self-called Nice People praise their own way of life, while condemning the residents of the opposite riverbank.

All this caused the outsider great distress, for he wanted desperately to find safety and security among friends, but did not know which side to choose. And something else was going on within him. A small voice advised him not to join either side. This voice seemed to come from something he had observed. He had observed—with both disappointment and shock—that both people were exactly the same—childish, hostile, scared.

The longer he delayed his choice, the greater grew his anxiety. But at a certain point, a curious thing happened. The energy aroused by his bewilderment suddenly became creative. He wondered whether there might be a place of residence above *both* communities. So exploring upstream, first on one bank and then on the other, he arrived at a beautiful expanse of land. It was situated high above both sides of the river. The outsider was pleased to find that at this height his loneliness had vanished completely. So in this peaceful region he built a home which he called "Above Both Sides." Whenever anyone asked why he had created this unusual name, he told them why.

Understand these great truths

Do you see the tremendous truth contained in this story? Connect it with the following paragraphs of comment. Go over and over the ideas until you sense their hidden depths. That sensing is the start of your new life.

Emotional pain occurs when you occupy a "yes" position and a "no" comes up, or when you occupy "no" and "yes" appears. "Yes" and "no" have no power for pain in themselves. Both form the naturally alternating flow of life, just as the ocean expresses itself with incoming and outgoing tides. We feel pain only when a misunderstanding of our true nature makes us cling to either "yes" or "no," while resisting its opposite. During the next hour, experiment by not resisting the natural swing from one side to the other, which means you will not fight what seems to be a threat to your present position.

Where is the enemy? At first we place it somewhere outside ourselves in the form of a stubborn circumstance or someone who opposes our wishes. Looking closer, we locate the enemy within, but mistakenly think it consists of incurable badness. Approaching even closer, we see that the enemy is nothing more than a wrong use of the mind. We see how we wrongly divided the mind into enemy and friend, into evil and good. It is our new wholeness which sees this, and this wholeness cannot find an enemy anywhere, for it now knows there is really nothing outside of its own wholeness.

It is contrast which wakes us up, not the usual. This is because contrast forces us to look, while we never notice the usual. So a contrast to our usual ways should be enthusiastically studied, whether it is the sudden ending of a friendship or a change in our financial conditions or anything else. The study and understanding of contrasts create a wondrous psychic stability. You will then observe contrasts in life, but never be shocked or hurt by them.

"Our need to simply understand is increasingly clear to me," said Arnold S., "so I would like to understand those times when I feel denied—denied anything at all." Answer: "Denial exists first as a word, then as a conditioned reflex, then as a pain, but never at any time as a reality. Examine this process for yourself and you will see the falsity of believing in denial. Cancel your supposed need for fulfillment and you also cancel denial, for one creates the other."

A man with false desires will attempt to satisfy them by going to wrong places and meeting wrong people. This always gets him into trouble in one way or another, but in his unawareness he may even call his approaching trouble a stroke of good fortune—until the inevitable shock occurs. We see this in the case of a lonely person whose heart thrills at meeting an attractive person of the opposite sex, only to sadly discover that he or she is just another smiling deceiver. We must study false desire intensely.

An unhappy person lives only from what he wants—what he wants to possess and what he wants to believe. Getting what he wants supplies a passing thrill; not getting his desires arouses anger and insecurity. He pursues what he thinks will make him happy, never noticing that what he thinks will make him happy never makes him happy. He can get off the merry-go-round of thrill-followed-by-depression by studying the true nature of happiness. Happiness is not *getting*, but *being*. Being what? Being who you really are.

ON THE ROAD TO DAMASCUS

A merchant was approaching Damascus when he heard a cry for help. At the side of the road he found a man injured by a fall into a ditch. Though not seriously hurt, he required assistance, which the merchant offered.

"Do you have five buttons on your coat?" inquired the injured man. Surprised by the question, the merchant asked about it. The man in the ditch answered, "All my life people have been telling me that good can only come from a man with five buttons on his coat." After groaning for a moment, the man spoke again to the merchant: "Tell me, have you ever seen a fox resting beneath a fig tree?"

"Why on earth do you want to know that?" asked the baffled merchant. Replied the injured man, "Because all my teachers have been telling me I must receive aid only from someone who has seen a fox resting beneath a fig tree."

Said the merchant, "You had better forget all that nonsense and listen to what your pain is now telling you."

Twenty cures for personal suffering

There is something both beautiful and amazing about the path we are now taking. In a flash, at this very instant, we can cut away fearful beliefs and foolish superstitions and see what we can do for ourselves. We can be aware of a personal and individual condition which needs correction—the condition of pain.

Human suffering can be ended. You can end your suffering, regardless of its persistence. But you must study yourself, not with a heavy spirit, but with the delight of an explorer who has discovered a new land. Fill your future days and months with an enthusiastic examination of the following basic facts about the cure for sorrow.

1. You are not required to believe in the heartache of yourself or of anyone else.
2. Self-pain can be evaded through emotionalism, dramatics, chatter, accusation, pretense, dependency, demands, daydreams—or self-pain can be faced and understood and ended.
3. Suffering is nothing more than the penalty for lack of self-knowledge, so when that knowledge is won, suffering is defeated.
4. When all we have left is our suffering, our opportunity for self-enlightenment is perfect, which we can then use by letting go of our last attachment—our suffering itself.
5. Just as an airplane has special equipment for studying a storm it flies through, so do you possess internal instruments for studying and understanding suffering.

6. To succeed in using grief to end grief, experience it directly, fully, consciously, without the interference of labels which call it "unjust" or "exciting" or "necessary."
7. Most people live from, "All will be well if nothing disturbs me," when we should live from, "What within me is unnecessarily disturbed?"
8. To accept reality does not mean to sullenly surrender to a superior force, but to realize that your true nature includes this other force, so acceptance means to accept your own wholeness, which is without frustration.
9. Suffering always runs along the tracks of mechanical thought, so by permitting consciousness to interrupt mechanical thought, we learn the secret for ending suffering.
10. To "let go" means to respond to a crisis with a wish to understand it, instead of arming ourselves with mechanical anger or habitual distress.
11. Even if you do not understand it, start right now to withdraw your consent to being hurt and deceived and confused, for total withdrawal of consent ends those conditions.
12. An exterior result can cause no pain unless something in the man insists that the result affirm his self-images, so it is imaginary self-pictures which cause pain, not results.
13. When the agony of protecting and promoting oneself in a hostile world becomes

unbearable, when the crisis reaches its peak—*that* is the opportunity for smashing through to self-liberty.

14. Rage and its accompanying pains can be cured by one method only—by receiving truths we do not want to receive.
15. Mental and emotional pain always include a stubborn self-will which opposes cosmic will, so it is clear that the ending of self-will is also the ending of pain.
16. When you are completely one with yourself you cannot have conflict or agony, which is why self-unity must be a primary aim.
17. In daily contacts with people and events, you can be just as swift toward composure as toward nervousness, for the swiftness will serve whichever you prefer.
18. Do not turn against yourself, no matter how badly you may have blundered in the past, for blundering exists only in man-made time, and your true nature does not live in time, but in the pure present.
19. Man's new and true nature remains comfortable with everything it encounters, just as a stream flows casually around every shape of rock.
20. Suffering instantly loses all power over the person who truly understands it—and it can be understood perfectly.

THE CONFUSED CONQUEROR

King Pyrrhus of Epirus was asked by his friend, Cineas, "Sir, if you conquer Rome, what will you do next?"

Pyrrhus replied, "Sicily is nearby, and will be easy to take."

"And what will you do after Sicily?" Cineas asked.

"Then we will pass over to Africa and plunder Carthage."

"And after Carthage?"

"After Carthage we will conquer Greece and Macedon."

Cineas inquired, "What do you expect as a reward from all these victories?"

"Then," said Pyrrhus, "we can sit down and enjoy ourselves."

"Can we not," suggested Cineas," enjoy ourselves now?"

There is no need to prove yourself

Cineas had grasped a fundamental fact about true living. He saw the necessity of living within the only time zone in existence—the present moment. Man blunders endlessly by trying to escape into future time, in trying to feel thrilled instead of wishing to feel right. It never occurs to him to inquire of himself, "Now that I've won, what have I won?"

Self-excellence begins when we glimpse how we have been unknowingly working against our true interests.

Floyd C. requested, "May we have an example of how we unconsciously work against our own deliverance?" Floyd wrote down this answer: "People go against themselves because of a false belief in what is required of them. To waste precious energy in chasing what frantic society calls good fortune is never required. You are never obligated to be on anyone's side but your own true side. You are not required to listen to discouragement."

The truly spiritual life does not include obligations. It is a dreary burden to feel obligated about anything at all, but to feel obligated to be decent or pleasant implies that one is *not* naturally decent or pleasant. It is altogether a ridiculous form of self-deception, but people love religious or social obligations for they can now say, "See, I obey the rules. Now I am owed something." How different is true spirituality, in which a free mind dwells above the burdens of feeling obligated and feeling owed.

A person can act either from an invented self-image or from his original nature. Chaos or harmony depends upon his selection. By acting from a flattering self-image of being successful or pleasant or authoritative, he finds himself opposed by everyone else with the same images. This is why "important" people secretly dislike other "important" people. Giving ourselves a label gives us neither identity nor security, and when this is seen, our action is pure action.

Suppose you have a friend who is nervously anxious to become a famous artist. One day you accompany him to an art contest in which each artist is given an hour to complete his drawing. As your friend works tensely, you decide to use the time to draw your own picture, which you do with casual enjoyment. Your relaxation is the same relaxation known by those who live in truth. They are active but casual, for they are free of the nagging ego which forces others to nervously try to prove themselves all day long.

A tractor might get loose and run wild over a field of vegetables, ruining everything it hits. But once that tractor stops, it cannot go again unless someone starts it. Here is the valuable lesson: destructive error has no power of its own. It cannot start itself. It runs wild repeatedly only when misunderstanding starts it again. Experiment with this at your first opportunity. If someone is rude to you, do not give it power over you by getting upset. Just understand the other man's self-damaging error.

Disorders are healed when lifted to a higher plane of thought than the plane which caused them, for on this higher plane we cease to interfere with the healing.

THE MAN WHO ENDED SELF-DAMAGE

For many years a man was puzzled by some peculiar happenings in his yard. On some mornings he discovered various damage, such as broken stems on a rose bush and uprooted grass. At first he blamed neighbors or roving animals but soon eliminated them as suspects. Thinking that mysterious psychic forces might be at work, he consulted a teacher of mystical wisdom. The teacher told him, "Yes, I know the cause, but you would not believe me if I told you, so you must see for yourself. I want you to awaken yourself in the middle of the night. Do just that much, then return here."

Though puzzled by the advice, the man followed it. To his astonishment, he awoke one night to find himself standing in his yard—damaging his own property. Upon returning to the wise man, he was told, "Unless you had experienced the shock of seeing this for yourself, you would never have known the truth. You see, unconscious negativities compel you to walk in your sleep, doing damage even while dreaming you are being constructive. Now that you are aware of this, I can show you how to stop damaging yourself."

What it means to be awake

Take a single principle and give it your wholehearted attention for an entire day. Here is a good one for a start: Knowledge of misfortune ends misfortune. When you truly understand the nature of adversity, it ceases to appear, for then the unconscious mind no longer produces negative forces which cause adverse effects. You can prove this for yourself by acquiring the necessary knowledge.

A man heard about a foreign country which was supposed to be the ideal place in which to live.

Visiting there, he was shocked to see widespread poverty and unhappiness. When asked why he did not settle there, he replied, "I saw what it was really like." Let this be a reminder of a first lesson in self-awakening—we must see what our life is really like, even if it upsets us a bit. When a teacher offers his aid in doing this, his purpose is not to hurt, but to heal.

Upon observing a fault in yourself, neither justify nor condemn it. To justify or condemn means you are using the habitual way of thinking, the mechanical way of thinking, which always divides everything into opposites, like justification and condemnation or right and wrong. Observe the fault from a *third viewpoint*, which is above these opposites, which frees you. The third viewpoint is quiet awareness.

You can ascend to the level where everything is seen directly, without interference from so-called human reasoning. This is the liberty level. For example, when seeing human hostility you need not try to figure out its cause. The only cause of any hostility is the empty and frightened nature of the hostile person. This perception will be equaled by the perception that human hostility is powerless to affect you.

You are quite capable of producing your own psychological atmosphere, which society's negative atmosphere cannot penetrate.

"You have already given us several definitions of what it means to be inwardly awake," said

Lew S., "but may we have another description of the awakened state?" Reply: "To be awake means to not suffer any more from anything. By remaining inwardly awake you will never fall into a painful nightmare. This need not be a mystery to you. It can be just as clear as the way you unfold a newspaper."

Only our own spiritual logic can convince us of anything. As an adventure in true logic, take paper and pencil and see how many ways you can state the following truth in your own words: *"Right and beneficial actions arise only from deep self-knowledge."* You might write, *"To see right is to do right,"* or *"Pure water comes from a pure spring."* This exercise makes *a* truth *your* truth.

WHAT HAPPENED AT THE OASIS

A Sufi teacher taught classes in an oasis of the Sahara Desert. One pupil had difficulty understanding a fact which every beginner must realize. He failed to see that the suppression of unhappiness is not the same thing as happiness. The teacher explained how most people suppress their distress by involvement in noisy and useless activities. The teacher then gazed out over the rolling sand dunes and asked the pupil, "Do you see that approaching horseman?"

The pupil looked out and answered, "Yes."

"Keep watching. Do you see him all the time?"

"No. He appears and disappears behind the sand dunes."

"When he disappears from sight, does he become happier than when be comes into view?"

"No. Wherever he goes, he is always the same man."

"Suppression of unhappiness is like that," the Sufi applied the lesson. "Hiding from conflict changes nothing; it can only make things worse. We never really deceive ourselves by putting on a mask of gaiety. Now knowing this, you can proceed to the next step. Become fully aware of how troubled and bewildered you really are. An intense self-honesty will lift you naturally up to the next step, and to the next and the next, until you stand free of yourself."

Truth is compassionate to all

Because the truth is gentle and kindly, it also shocks. It has no motive in shocking except to awaken suffering humanity. Falsehood fears to shock, for its selfish interests require sleeping people to remain asleep, therefore falsehood is ruthless and cruel. Knowing its own innocence, truth can say, "Sacrifice to others in hope of securing their support for your shaky self-structure can only bring heartache. That wonderful person you idolize is just as lost as you are. Do not call evil good. Let that begin your self-rescue."

Self-battling is the perfect description of the unaware man. Take his feelings toward his neighbor. In rapid succession he is taken over by feelings of pretended friendliness, by feelings of actual hostility, by feelings dictated by moral codes, by feelings prompted by a guilty conscience and so on. No wonder he feels like a trapped soldier on a battlefield! His first duty is to become shockingly aware of his actual condition, which makes further progress possible.

Make it your aim to discover how you truly feel about something or someone at the precise moment of the feeling. Do not consider how you *should* feel. To see clearly, tolerate no veils of habitual thought. Above all, we must see what we are like at any particular moment. Irritation must be seen as irritation and not covered over with a self-pleasing label. This practice ends division between the actual and the unreal, making us whole.

"You say we must not protect ourselves against disgrace," stated Joyce W. "This is startling. I'd like to know what it means." Reply: "Why should you protect yourself against disgrace? So you can suffer some more? Look. You feel disgrace when some sugar-sweet idea you have about yourself is shaken by reality. For example, your husband might gently suggest you are not as wise in financial matters as you like to think you are. Facts in themselves never cause disgrace; it is our anxious self-protection which makes us feel bad. When you don't protect, you don't suffer."

You must not condemn yourself for anything, which does not mean to abandon self-responsibility. Condemnation prevents understanding. Try to see why. At the moment of condemnation, you are not the same person who may have behaved unwisely one second or fifty years ago. You are new every second, but mistakenly think you possess a fixed personality. So when you condemn, you condemn a mere memory about yourself, which is pointless. By living with your moment-by-moment newness, you banish the tyranny of a memorized self. Your understanding of this makes you blameless, for it breaks the mechanical repetition of unwise behavior, and replaces it with conscious goodness.

To say that goodness is its own reward is not merely a moral teaching; it is a solid psychological fact. We should be good not because of the urgings of an exterior teacher, but because we hear and understand the wisdom of our inner teacher. Be a perceptive human being who really understands this simple teaching: "Be good and you will feel good." Such a person is truly good because he has no other nature than that of Cosmic Goodness.

Just as medical scientists discover new cures for physical illness, so do your investigations reveal new psychic medicines which cure all of life.

INSPIRATIONS FROM CHAPTER SIX

1. Learn to think in a new way about human anguish.
2. Personal suffering can be ended completely.
3. We must study the actual nature of inner conflict.

End Pain and Anxiety

4. Let consciousness replace mechanical thinking.
5. You need not consent to hurt feelings.
6. There is no need to prove or to protect yourself.
7. The awakened mind does not suffer from anything.
8. We must abolish unhappiness, not merely suppress it.
9. The mission of truth is to heal, not to hurt.
10. You now possess powers for ending personal pain.

7

Release the Power of Your Higher Mind

THE SEVENTH BELL

A farming village in the mountains of Germany needed a swift and simple method for calling its scattered citizens together. Deciding to install a large bell inside the town's highest tower, the people authorized their mayor to find the right bell for their needs. Journeying to a large city having many bell-makers, the mayor made his first call. When shown a belt having many attractive designs, he asked to hear its tone. Not attracted to what he heard, the mayor went on to the next bell-maker on his list, but something about the second bell was also not quite right. When declining to approve the tone of the third bell, he was asked what was wrong. "I know what I want," replied the prudent mayor, "but I have not heard it as yet." Eventually, when hearing the seventh bell, he asked to hear its tones a few more times. Listening closely, he nodded in satisfaction. The mayor knew he had found a bell with the unique power and clearness for bringing his people together.

The true meaning of bravery

Have you ever noticed that you may not have found what you are seeking? Notice it right now. This clear noticing is an act of intelligence. Say to yourself, "Up to now I have been seeking in the wrong directions. This is obvious enough, for I have found nothing which satisfies." Permit yourself to see this fact even more deeply; let it shock you if it wishes. This will awaken something dynamic within. Even if you are somewhat hazy about it, this fact is not hazy; it knows how to work for you and will do so. Then, like the mayor, you will recognize that true tone you have always wanted to hear.

So much depends upon our listening habits, whether we listen to noisy inner voices which demand victories in society, or to that other voice which invites victory over ourselves.

Anyone who has begun to recognize truth when he hears it can be of great aid to timid beginners.

Such a man was Ben H., who said, "At the start I feared that these principles required me to abandon my common sense. As if I had any! After realizing all my past folly I wonder whether I ever had one ounce of sense in my head. Now I see why we must first abandon the illusion that we know what we are doing with our lives." Ben is definitely on his way to authentic intelligence.

What keeps a man under the hypnotic belief that he is doing the best he can for himself? It is his surrounding of himself with people who think as he thinks, who harm themselves in the same way he harms himself. He takes every precaution to avoid stepping out of his familiar circle, for that would cause anxiety. But he must dare to do without the reassurance of the familiar, for that will shatter his prison-circle. This will provide his first experience with something outside of himself, and when feeling it, his personal miracle has begun.

Say to yourself, "From this moment on I will do what I sense is truly right, regardless of the consequences." The consequences can never be bad for your true nature, though it may appear so at the time. The truly brave man is the one who dares everything for the sake of his own liberation. See how much you can get away with by not sacrificing your psychic freedom to others. You will be amazed at how far you can go.

Curiously, the first mile of the true path is paved with intense dissatisfactions with the old paths. A right kind of dissatisfaction with our thinking comes by observing that our thoughts always occupy the same level as our unhappiness, that our present thinking *is* our unhappiness. This is a powerful incentive for seeking and possessing that great treasure—a free and happy mind.

The start of our new life is like hearing the distant roar of ocean waves which cannot be seen as yet. But as we push aside obstacles in our path, the entire scene appears, providing a clear view of waves, ships, passengers and all else. People want to know, "How will we feel when attaining the full vision of life?" American author Herman Melville answers, *"It is a very fine feeling, and one that fuses us into the universe of things, and makes us part of the All."*

HOW THE WATER BECAME PURE

A refugee of ancient Babylon came upon a fresh countryside, which he believed would be excellent for a new home for himself and his family. Taking a large jar, he searched around the hills and valleys for a source of pure water. He found several springs and streams, but when the water was used at the family camp it tasted bitter. Unwilling to leave his new home, he sat down to calmly ponder the problem. His orderly thinking led to an experiment, which led to a discovery. The water was pure at its source, but had been made bitter by the impure jar from the old country. When using a new jar, he found all waters pure and healthy.

You can uplift your inner nature

Our inner nature, whether positive or negative, always duplicates itself for happiness or sorrow in the exterior life. We do not receive according to what we say we want, but according to the level—high or low—of the unseen, unconscious and unspoken request.

If you spent the next ten years studying this single idea, you would have an enormously profitable investment.

It is our deep and actual nature which determines whether our contacts with life will be healthy or disorderly. So it is the depths which we must explore, while never giving value to surface personality. A seeker asked a teacher, "How can I meet life's challenges rightly?" The teacher told him, "You answer life with your own nature, for that is the only answer you have."

How can we begin to change our nature in order to answer with full power and health?

Imagine yourself seated in a home where a small child is playing with a ball. The child suddenly hurls the ball through the air toward a vase. You leap up and halt the path of the ball, thus saving the vase. With diligent practice you can stop thoughts which would otherwise hurtle forwards to cause psychic and physical destruction. This success comes when you alertly watch your own thoughts, then remember the law of cause and effect.

If a man really understood the scientific fact that he gets what he unconsciously gives, would that man be content to remain as he is?

Gordon A. asked, "How can I stop doing things which at the time seem right, but which turn around and punish me?" Reply: "Whenever you perform an act of any kind, try to be aware of your state of mind which produced that act. Among other values, you will see a deeper working of the law of cause and effect."

You can make an experiment which may seem strange at first, but which turns into pure delight. Simply proceed through your day as if nothing harmful can ever happen to you by choosing what is true and right, which is a fact. Sometimes we hesitate before rightness, for fear of some disadvantage. Something will happen to the false sense of self all right—it will lose its grip on us, and the small shock we feel when choosing rightness is just its protest over losing power over us. Regardless of how it seems, nothing but goodness can ever come by choosing goodness.

You must remind yourself that every circumstance can remain a neutral circumstance and not turn into a personal problem. Do this in two steps:

1. Realize that it is the conditioned mind which divides everything into good or bad.
2. Think from above these opposites, which is quite possible and an amazing experience.

Cease to think of the future in terms of events, either favorable or unfavorable. That is useless. Think of the future in terms of yourself, of your inner state. You are your own future. Realizing this, will you try to influence events, or will you influence your thoughts and feelings toward trueness? Your opportunities for this self-work are limitless, for there is no time when you are not with yourself.

The truth is a single unit which expresses itself in various ways, just as a single tree expresses fruit and color and size. So the seeing of one fact draws your mental eyes toward another nearby fact. See another's arrogance as a sign of weakness and you can also see why arrogance need not intimidate you. See what it means to be self-acquainted and you can also feel the comfort of being at home with yourself.

Keep everything uncomplicated, including your collection of knowledge. If you want an automobile to work for you, you must acquire knowledge of how it works. So it is with the services offered by your inner self. The powers you already possess will surely work for you when understood and released. Just do not complicate things with unnecessary motions, such as worry over results.

THE SHIPWRECKED SAILOR

A sailor was shipwrecked on a lonely and remote island in the Pacific Ocean. Knowing he would probably be stranded there for a long time, he wisely set about to provide for himself. Among the wreckage washed ashore from his ship he found a wide variety of vegetable seeds. While having scant knowledge of gardening, he realized the value of experimentation. Accordingly, he planted all the seeds, including those for carrots, lettuce, corn and cabbage. By working and watching, his knowledge and skill increased swiftly. He discovered which vegetables were natural to the island's soil and which were not. This enabled him to cease to waste himself on useless seeds, and to give full time and attention to seeds having practical value. This wise procedure gave him more than enough food to survive until rescued.

How to keep a fresh and healthy mind

To see what is true, see what is untrue. That is a basic tool for building another kind of life. You could see it is untrue that the average human being is a single, unified, consistent person. He changes his roles a dozen times a day, rarely noticing it. A person can be very sweet and helpful as long as he wants something, but after getting what he wants you may see an entirely different person before you. Today, see something which is definitely untrue, for that is positive self-work.

Even a single seed of mental honesty has a delightful way of producing many desirable fruits. Perhaps the seed is the wish to see the difference between false appearances of rightness and authentic rightness based on invisible cosmic principles. The power of this wish springs into immediate action. It reveals why friendships often end in quarrels—because both parties live from roles, not realities. Then, the observer learns to love realities, not roles, which sets him free from surrounding falseness.

Your Higher Mind

Whenever a thought of any kind appears in your mind, observe its nature and let it fade away. This is the mind's natural way, which keeps you fresh and healthy. If a negative thought appears, do not cling to it in order to prolong its peculiar thrill. That is blockage and self-injury, which few human beings see as injury because they call it excitement. Your mind should flow like a river, free and unobstructed, and when it does, your life as a whole will flow with equal ease.

As self-observation does its good work, we understand more and more the esoteric saying, "It is good to see the bad." Our uncovered negativities become less of a shock and more of a condition to be eliminated. We are even delighted to see the extent of our confusion, for we know that a correct diagnosis of the illness is a healthy part of the cure. People who dwell in dreamland never see their actual condition, and so remain victims of themselves. You and I are not going to live like that.

Unconscious wrongness is the prison cell; consciousness of wrongness is the key.

"You stress the necessity for making the unconscious conscious, which I understand," said Ralph M., "for we just don't see what we are doing against ourselves. Please show us one unconscious area we must expose and banish." Reply: "If only we would stop dramatizing ourselves, either before others or in our own imaginative mental films, what a blow for freedom that would be!"

Archaeologists have dug through layer after layer

of Jericho and other ancient cities to discover the character of their former civilizations. This illustrates our course. Do we have hidden motives or desires or guilts? All can be understood and handled if only we will expose them to the light of consciousness. No underground characteristic need remain a source of mystery and anguish.

We must let reality gently pull us away from our fearful insistence that everything must remain as it is. That is the same as saying we must let contentment replace discontent. Even when we protest, we must fall forward while protesting. No one is going to condemn us for crying out, for there is no one in existence to condemn, so we need not feel ashamed of our timidity. Psychic prisoners need to see and feel one fact; the truth is not hauling them off to a deeper dungeon, but to the liberty of the front gate.

THE BATTERED VILLAGE

There was once a village with the sea at its front and the jungle at its back. It was a primitive village, far removed from the more advanced cities of the country. Every few months the area was battered by rains and hurricanes. The villagers adjusted as best they could to the recurring damage. But one month a storm of severe intensity swept down on the town. Gathering up their belongings, the natives attemped to flee, but found themselves blocked. The usual roads leading inland were washed out.

Hearing of the disaster, the capital city sent airplanes which scattered instructive leaflets down on the desperate people. The leaflets revealed an unfamiliar but entirely safe route of escape.

But there was a problem. Most of the villagers had never taken time to learn the language of their own country. They could only stare in bewilderment at the instructions which could save them. Fortunately, there were a few citizens who understood the language. They eagerly explained the message to those who could not read. But strangely, many listeners distrusted these helpful people, even accusing them of leading the people astray.

But sensing something true about the explanation, some villagers took the revealed route to safety and to relief.

Follow these pathways to progress

Perhaps you see in this story the main message of Truth:

1. Man is trapped by his own stormy nature.
2. By listening patiently to the message from a higher plane, he rescues himself.

All who have found their way out of the human jungle have started by reflecting, "Perhaps another way exists." It does.

You learn a lot by listening to what a true teacher talks about, but wisdom is also gathered by noticing what he does *not* talk about. He refuses to discuss man-made schemes by which one group of people can get the best of another group. He has nothing to do with talk about a happiness based on excitement or acquisition. The teacher knows the impossibility of creating jewels out of junk.

How can you check the credentials of a teacher? There is only one way. We must have at least a single ray of light in ourselves, for it is that light which reveals the authenticity of a teacher. People without this light would ask Christ whether he had a college degree in psychology, or ask Buddha whether he had read the latest theories of a noted professor of sociology. Some day you may meet a man who knows what he is talking about. To make sure you don't walk right past him without sensing his trueness, brighten your own light right now.

Proceed with the assurance of reaching right conclusions. However, never make conclusions yourself, instead, let them come to you, which they will do when traditional conclusions are kept out. We have discussed the value of being honest and open about our actual condition, whatever it may be. By doing this the right conclusion comes. Where there is no hiding there can be no hurting, for hiding and hurting fight it out in the same dark closet.

People ask, "How will I know I am building a more mature mind?" They will know. Maturity is its own evidence. There are small signs at first. Paul E. used to get disturbed when unexpected obstacles slowed down a business plan. But during one particular delay he saw himself standing apart from the impatient reactions which formerly captured him. He was pleased at this sign of progress.

We need have no concern regarding the source of new strength and wisdom for the tasks ahead. They will keep pace with us. The railroads of the early West pushed across the prairies with supplies carried forward by rails already laid. By doing what is right for today, we need take no thought for tomorrow.

Suppose an ornithologist wants to study the nesting activities of various birds. To make his studies without disturbing the birds, he climbs to the lower part of a tree next to the tree with the nests. Gazing over, he studies a nest. Wishing to study a higher nest, he himself climbs upward and again looks over. We must do likewise in our studies. It is our upward climb from our present psychic position which makes higher ideas understandable.

Declare to yourself, "Nothing in life has any meaning except my aim to wake up, to see life as it really is. So whatever my daily duties, I will use every minute, every thought, every energy to achieve this aim." Now, if you succeed just one-tenth of one percent at first, that is tremendous!

THE BIRDS WHO REFUSED TO FLY

A visitor to the farmlands was surprised by what he saw in a certain location. Off to the side of the road was a meadow, not more than a mile or two wide. Crowded into the space were hundreds of birds of every kind and every size. The birds were obviously nervous and irritable. When reaching the farm of his friend, the visitor asked about the strange situation: "Why are those birds so closely confined in that limited space? I see no fence to keep them in."

The farmer told this story: "Many years ago a pitiless landowner captured hundreds of birds and placed them in the meadow you saw. A high fence was erected and armed guards were posted to prevent escape. The landowner gained a twisted pleasure from having power over the wild creatures. Later, when the man moved away, the guards disappeared and the fence fell down. But by this time the birds had acquired a fence-mentality, which they passed on to their children. Oddly, the birds now believe that the meadow is their freedom and that the open space beyond the meadow is a place of imprisonment. So they refuse to fly away. Many good men have tried to reveal the truth to the birds, but ignorance causes fear, and fear causes hostility, so many good men have been attacked in the meadow."

The farmer concluded his story: "Men who understand what happened to the birds still come out here. They try to teach the unhappy creatures that the fence exists only in the wrong working of their minds. But you can see for yourself what patient persistence it takes."

Live from your own free mind

This story can be summarized: Because men and women misunderstand, they fear their own freedom, and thus block their rightful happiness.

A teacher wished to impress a first lesson upon a new group of seekers. Calling them together, he declared, "You are unhappy, but you don't have to remain unhappy. You are a slave to anger, but you need not remain a slave. You are in a constant state of nervousness, but it is not necessary to remain nervous." He concluded, "Those of you who wish to know more, please come at once to my school in the woods." Without giving further directions, he disappeared. The right to know more was earned by those who exerted themselves enough to find the school.

"I am familiar with many basic truths," said Jean E., "but something is wrong. For instance, I know I must do my own thinking, but I am still wrongly influenced by others. Why?" Reply: "Because you know it as a quotation but not as a personal experience. Ponder deeply the difference in the two. Anyone can quote. The personal experience comes through abandonment—first the abandonment *of* human opinion and then the abandonment *to* cosmic fact."

One troubled inquirer was told, "The reason you trade your mental integrity to others in exchange for what you want from them is because you think you must do so. You do not know that you need not do so. But you can know, and then you will see."

When we behave as if we need not sacrifice our mental integrity to anyone, it produces uncertainty at first but feels right at last. This is always a great moment in our upward journey, for we have dared to let go of our false security to enter and to examine the uncertain unknown. Then, that unknown, that strange emptiness, produces a marvelous change which words cannot describe, but which is real.

To encourage his students to empty themselves of false values, a teacher asked, "If a treasure chest is filled with stones, can you add jewels?"

Human beings fear the freedom of thinking for themselves. "How will we know what to do unless someone tells us?" They ask in bewilderment, "How can we live without traditional beliefs and sacred institutions?" No one ever thinks to ask, "*Are* we living, or only agitating?" Ask a patient hospitalized for months where his freedom is and he will tell you, "Anywhere outside."

Ralph Waldo Emerson explained, *"The difficulty is that we do not make a world of our own, but fall into institutions already made."* A man joins this or that group in a frantic effort to feel secure, but when the crowd vanishes, so does his assurance. This man has the bad habit of seeing things which don't exist, which is not the habit of an informed mind. The lesson: "Live from yourself. An artificial flower cannot grow."

THE RESOLUTE LISTENER

Parmenides was a Greek philosopher who taught that the being of man is changeless, eternal and one with the universe. He set down his advanced teachings in his poem, *On Nature*, which advocated right thinking. Parmenides had much to give to whoever wanted to receive his wisdom.

On one occasion, when Parmenides was lecturing on the truths he had discovered, he looked out to see only one listener left in the audience. Only one inquirer had sufficient interest and enthusiasm to listen to the details of the wisdom of the ages. That one man who wanted to hear the truth more than he wanted anything else became a famous philosopher himself. His name was Plato.

The secret of secrets

What have you placed first in your life? Think about it, even as you hold this book. Now inquire whether this primary objective has delivered true and lasting satisfaction. What is your conclusion?

As Plato realized, only one objective has lasting value. That objective is to become one with our own original nature. Among other values, it ends anxious efforts in life.

Anxious efforts to keep the exterior world in place according to personal demand are useless and impossible. Whoever is caught in this conflict can free himself by understanding what it means to keep the world in place. As Wayne T. was told, "Learn to keep yourself in place and there will be no other world with which to struggle. To be one with yourself, in harmony with yourself, is the same thing as being in unified harmony with the world."

Thoughts come to your mind for hundreds of beneficial purposes, including efficiency in daily tasks and command of the emotions. Non-interference with their original pure flow permits the accomplishment of their good purposes. Harmful interference consists of negative thoughts which fail to understand the helpful intentions of original thoughts. Perhaps a man is informed of his unnatural behavior. This pure thought is received, but then distorted by resentment, so the man remains uncorrected. So thought-study is vital. If you want to know which flowers in a garden have perfume and which do not, come close to them.

To think correctly, and therefore beneficially, we must understand how the mind actually operates. Examine these two major movements:

1. Consciousness
2. Thought

Consciousness, or awareness, is clear perception which sees things as they are. It is timeless and without division. It does not divide life into yesterday and tomorrow, into you and I, into German and Frenchman, into God and man. Consciousness is intelligence, freedom, sanity.

Thought dwells in time, and divides everything into opposites, as shown in the above examples.

But there are two kinds of thought, which can be defined as follows:

(a) Practical thought

(b) Negative thought

We employ practical thought when conducting business, when driving a car or cooking dinner or doing any of the dozens of usual tasks in our day.

This is the correct use of thought, for it serves practical purposes.

Negative thought is any thought which is self-damaging, which is foreign to our true nature, and which takes us away from either consciousness or practical thought. Examples: Daydreaming, fear, self-pity, resentment, vanity, self-deception, jealousy.

A healthy, happy and awakened mind alternates naturally between consciousness and practical thought.

An unhappy and self-punishing mind alternates between practical thought and negative thought.

Watch your own mind and the minds of other people just to see how true this is. Once this is seen clearly, your life changes swiftly and delightfully, for this is the secret of secrets.

As an aid, write the following guide upon a slip of paper, then read it and ponder it several times during the day: "My mind should never be in negative thought, but only in consciousness or in practical thought."

LIVE WITH THESE PRACTICAL IDEAS

1. We must listen carefully to our true nature.
2. The consequences of choosing truth are always good.
3. Our inner nature reproduces itself in the outer world.

4. Your opportunities for inner advancement are limitless.
5. To see what is true—that is our goal.
6. Let your mind flow easily, casually, naturally.
7. You will be able to see and feel your own progress.
8. Aim to know the truth by personal experience.
9. You need not trade your mental integrity to anyone.
10. Learn about and harmonize with your own mind.

8

The Path to Permanent Self-Command

THE PUZZLED PORCUPINES

There was once a community of porcupines who lived in a cold country. In order to escape the wintry weather, they agreed upon a plan of action. So on the next particularly cold day they came together and huddled as closely as possible. At first it looked like an ideal arrangement, but a problem soon arose. Their very closeness caused them to poke at each other with their sharp quills, making everyone pained and irritated. So the plan was canceled, with each porcupine going his separate way. But the coldness was so distressing they were forced to meet and huddle once more, and once more they poked and injured each other. So because they knew of no other way, the confused porcupines repeated over and over the painful pattern of huddling, stabbing, dispersing and huddling once more.

How to live your own life

The porcupine story was the way philosopher Arthur Schopenhauer explained the tragic human condition. But far from being pessimistic about it, Schopenhauer cheerfully declared, "If a man will generate his own heat, he will be independent, he will be free of the conflict and pain which others must endure."

Man is deluded into thinking he can find self-security in people and possessions and in social causes. But the very fences he builds to confine his security are the very fences which limit the liberty which exists outside his pseudo-security. Because he never studies the nature of his confinement, he depends and he demands, he suffers and he weeps.

During a class discussion on authentic independence, the following points helped the class: "Dependency always creates unhealthy demands. The demands may be cunningly concealed, but they are always there. If we depend upon another person for our happiness or security, we will demand that he continue to serve us, or demand an increase in service. Everything about this is harmful. Self-dependence removes the harm."

Whenever you believe you possess security, identify the sources of your confidence. They might consist of a comfortable family life or perhaps in the fact that all is presently going well in general. If any source can change or be lost, no security exists in them, for there will be worried sensing of a possible upset in your routines. The only true source of security is in your own oneness with yourself, which is the same as Oneness with everything else, for that can never change or be lost.

Understand that the confining rules of the game exist within you, not outside. You can unknowingly block your own life-liberty, but other people are powerless to restrain you. Understand this and you can shatter all the rules of the painful game you no longer wish to play.

"I sense the rightness of these principles," stated Stuart L., "but what about those times when we feel we are falling?" Reply: "It is a sign of progress to feel you are falling! Students often feel they are losing control, when in fact they are losing the illusion of having had control. Your home is briefly empty between the moving out of old furniture and moving in of the new. You are feeling this temporary emptiness, which makes room for the new. Recall this fact whenever you feel uncertain."

When you are depending upon a person or a position for security, it is very good for you when this dependency is lost. Nothing better could happen to you, though the shock of the loss will try to tell you otherwise. The loss of an exterior support is an opportunity to also lose the unconscious anxiety involved in dependency. You should gratefully work with the opportunity.

A novel by Edward Bulwer-Lytton tells of a lonely visitor to London who walks daily through its noisy streets. After a few days he ceases to yearn for the green fields of his home. His injurious experience is described by William Wordsworth: *"The world is too much with us."* Part of our work is to remember the psychic green fields which await the world-weary person who wishes to return to them. This remembering becomes increasingly stronger as we shun exterior attractions, as we live not from the outer to the inner, but from the inner to the outer.

THE LESSON OF THE LEMON

A teacher of secret wisdom had established his school on an island off the coast of Australia. Every few months a new class was formed, composed of students from every continent. After hearing preliminary lessons, including the need for attentiveness, the class received a visual lesson. A vase of water with a lemon floating in it was set on a table. The teacher instructed a student, "Get rid of the lemon. Do this by pushing it to the bottom of the vase. Then, withdraw your hand."

The student followed instructions. When he withdrew his hand, the lemon rose to its original position on top of the water. A second pupil was instructed, "Get rid of the lemon by pushing it into the water out of sight. Then, release it." The lemon disappeared into the depths of the jar, but popped up once more in view of everyone.

"That is the first thing to notice about the nature of this lemon," said the teacher. "Push it down and it jumps up every time." A third student was instructed, "Get rid of the lemon by removing it from the jar altogether."

The student lifted the lemon and set it on the table, after which the teacher applied the lesson. "A lemon suppressed in a jar is still in a jar—and it is still sour. But removing it altogether is quite another process. Millions of people suffer needlessly because they do not see the difference between suppressing a negative state and removing it with self-knowledge."

How to overcome the world

Authentic self-command is a natural result of self-knowledge. Whoever knows himself commands himself, and does so effortlessly.

As a simple guide, remember that psychic health consists of everything which is conscious, while unhealth is everything which is suppressed into unconscious mental layers. Any attempt to make the unconscious conscious is healthy.

Max S. asked, "What is the difference between a conscious and an unconscious response to daily events?" Reply: "Suppose you are doing business with a stranger who has a hard face and a disapproving manner. An unconscious response, dictated by past experiences with hard people, arouses your anxiety or hostility, or perhaps a forced smile to cover up your tension. A conscious response, which lives only in the free present, is to see before you a scared human being, one with no power to arouse anything but your quiet understanding."

Our aim is to escape exterior influences of which we are unaware and place ourselves under conscious self-influences. Examples of each will aid our aim.

Exterior influences:

1. Laughing merely because others laugh.
2. Feeling uneasy over another person's disapproval.
3. Behaving as we think we are expected to behave.

Self-influences:

1. Listening for the truth from our own nature.
2. Refusing to let others make us feel guilty.
3. Studying with the wish to win self-command.

There is a party game in which a player closes his eyes, takes a spoon and tries to scoop up balls of cotton from a table. The lightness of the cotton makes it difficult for him to feel what he is doing, so the attempt is amusingly frustrating. A man's lack of mental sight similarly frustrates his attempts to do what is right for himself. It is the use of the new power of consciousness which shows him what to do. At this point he begins to understand how it is possible to enter zestfully into all of life without having self-concern.

Permanent Self-Command

We can be attracted toward the better life by two forces—by an outside force or by the truth-loving force within us. If a person is attracted merely by hearing a dynamic message of truth from another, he may lose interest a short time later. So the superior and steadfast attraction is that which arises from within. By doing everything possible to love what is truly right, our attraction toward our own deliverance increases daily.

To overcome yourself is the very same thing as overcoming the world.

THE EMPEROR OF GEMS

There was once a gem collector who was so successful he was known as the Emperor of Gems. Among his treasures were rubies from Burma, brilliant sapphires from Ceylon, Egyptian emeralds and glittering diamonds worthy of a king's crown.

Many people asked the emperor for advice for duplicating his success. All were given the same counsel: "Preliminary work is necessary. Mainly, you must study to learn the difference between true gems and false ones, for the world is filled with deceivers." The inquirers were then assigned challenging tasks which would teach them the necessary lessons. They were required to journey through foreign lands with strange customs, to endure stormy seas and to experience uncertain situations.

On one occasion, fifty men returned to tell the emperor they had done all which had been required of them. "May we now consider ourselves to be gem experts?" asked their spokesman.

"Each of you will answer that question for yourself in just a few minutes," replied their teacher. "But first let me ask you something. Did you notice that I never questioned your sincerity while you were working? It had to be this way because only you can tell whether you were sincere or not. We will now see whether you carried out my instructions out of mechanical duty or whether you did them because you deeply wanted to know a real gem when you saw one."

The men were then led into another room. Resting upon a velvet-covered table were hundreds of stones of every shape and color. "Examine these," said the emperor, "and tell me which are genuine and which are artificial. Do not consult with each other, for the man you ask may be quite wrong. Each man must answer for himself."

As the Emperor of Gems had predicted, each man became his own test. Only those who truly loved higher knowledge received a reward. The rich reward was the ability to collect an authentic gem whenever one was sighted.

Gems of esoteric thought

1. A change of mind is everything, as when changing the mind about what is truly good for us.
2. The only way to change what you see in life is to change the person doing the seeing, for you are what you see.

3. Any time you are unhappy, instantly realize it is a wrong thought which is unhappy, not the essential you.
4. One way to explain our daily task is to say we must replace self-desertion with self-return.
5. Control of yourself and of your life means one thing and one thing only—oneness with your self and with your life.
6. For benefit or for harm, the invisible thought produces the visible action.
7. For the next few minutes, do nothing but watch your thoughts and responses and physical movements, with no purpose in mind but to become acquainted with them.
8. The sure way to do something for your future is to do something with your present.
9. Only a person who has made sense of himself can make sense of the surrounding world.
10. Never believe that the limits of thought are the limits of the kingdom you can possess, for that positive disbelief reveals your limitless kingdom.
11. When you are truly in command of yourself, all anxious thoughts about command over men and events are absent, leaving you in command of your own happiness.
12. When within a crisis which seems to have no answer, remember the existence of cosmic consciousness in which no answer is needed.
13. We can use religious or psychological phrases

if we wish, or we can simply say our task is to get out of our own way.

14. You need cling to nothing except to your resolve to make complete sense out of life.
15. Practice these principles with no concern for results, for a planted seed is quite capable of developing in the dark.

THE TRAVELER WHO NEVER STOPPED

A traveler through the countryside was suddenly accosted by another traveler who told him in a frightened voice, "We have wasted our time in this direction. Behind those clouds is a vast mountain which will block our way."

Surprised at the report, the traveler set out to see whether it was true or not. He saw no mountain, but he did meet another stranger who gave him the gloomy report, "It is hopeless to continue your journey. Just beyond that meadow is a canyon so wide that even the animals are stopped by its edge."

Deciding to see for himself, the traveler went on his way. He saw that there was no canyon at all, but he did run into a third stranger in a military uniform, who sternly commanded, "Stop. You are forbidden to go on. This path leads straight into the camp of an army which will punish your attempts to continue."

Not frightened by the threat, the traveler walked on. There were no soldiers to block his way. So because the wise traveler decided to take no one's word for anything, but to test everything for himself, he was able to travel on and on and on.

The path to true confidence

The psychic traveler need not fear nor hesitate when meeting strange things which try to block his journey. Simply be aware that they are there—both inside you and outside—and walk right past them. Be like the hero in John Bunyan's classic allegory, *The Pilgrim's Progress*, who met and left behind dozens of tempters. Remember two facts:

1. They have no real power over you.
2. You can pass beyond every one of them, and walk on and on and on.

A secretary asked at her fifth class session: "May we hear more about discouragement? I need the information!" Reply: "Discouragement is absolutely nothing but a lack of self-understanding. Never think of it in any other way. Seeing discouragement in this way ends useless attempts at banishing it, such as rushing out to buy something, something you probably don't need anyway. Now seeing that discouragement is simply a lack of self-insight, you also see the cure."

"Have confidence in yourself" is popular advice with both a false and a true meaning. It depends upon what is meant by the "self." If it means a seemingly separate personality which seeks power over others, which is always demanding something, the advice becomes just another road to ruin. But if we take the self to mean an awakening point of cosmic consciousness, which steadily expands its vision of reality, the advice is accurate and inspiring.

The diligent traveler will see himself change before his own eyes. The wish to dominate is replaced by a wish to explore; no longer does he want to make a good impression, but to make a mental transformation; the desire to possess gives way to detached enjoyment. Such a student is beginning to see that true life consists of living with another self, with another viewpoint, another aim, another affection.

You can fly from the United States to Canada only by connecting yourself with the actual flight, not by discussing the flight with others. This applies also to the inner excursion. If only the surface part of the mind accepts self-involvement, there is no flight. Our connection with higher facts must be personal and individual, not social and interdependent. Become aware of the difference in the two ways.

Practice self-correction regularly. When something goes wrong, search out its cause within yourself. Dennis J. reported, "I still wrongly believe that people and events can fulfil me." Linda V. discovered, "I continually make the mistake of seeing myself as worthless instead of seeing myself as unaware." Marshall C. explained, "I neglect the overwhelming importance of giving everything I have to self-awakening."

A king's servant secretly tried on the king's crown,

to find it fitted exactly. Later, he was found to be the long-lost heir to the throne. Think of your mind as a king. That is its rightful title. But careless man has abdicated his rightful royalty because he thinks a peasant's life is all there is. By right work we can restore the mind to its kingly authority.

THE BUSINESSMAN'S RETURN

A successful businessman owned a fine home which was surrounded by acres of fruit trees. Every season he gathered an abundant harvest of apples and peaches and cherries. While on a business trip to a foreign country, he fell ill. Too weak to travel back home for a while, he wrote to some acquaintances who lived in a city not too far from his home. He asked them to take care of his property, granting permission for them to live in his home if they so desired. Accepting the invitation, the acquaintances moved in, promising to take care of everything.

While slowly recovering, the businessman wrote to his home, asking its occupants how things were going. He was assured that all was well, that while minor problems came up from time to time, there was nothing to worry about. The occupants seemed eager to convince the businessman that there was no need to hurry home, that his property was in good hands.

Sensing something wrong, the businessman made a successful effort to gain strength enough to return home. Upon arriving, his suspicions proved to be accurate. The careless and deceitful occupants had let home and orchard run down. He knew they had deceived him in order to continue to live at his expense. So regaining command of his own property, he soon restored its original attractiveness.

How to command your circumstances

How does this apply to us? Every man possesses an original psychic home of unique attractiveness. However, because of his departure to foreign lands, where he falls ill, he loses command of his home. Because of his separation he cannot see things as they really are, and so falls victim to cunning deceivers. For example, because he is anxious he is also gullible, and so follows anyone who wears a mask of authority and assurance.

A person finding himself absent from himself can know what to do. He can arouse himself, and like the Prodigal Son, make his way back home. Once regaining self-command, command of his circumstances follows naturally. And what does it mean to command circumstances? It does not mean to dominate them by surface personality or through human laws or with subtle or open threats. It means to have so dissolved false personality that you are in oneness with all your circumstances. Think deeply about this, then connect it with the next three paragraphs.

An event cannot produce a negative feeling unless that event contradicts a label we have unconsciously given ourselves. If Mr. X does not label himself as an original thinker, he will not be offended when told he lives by second-hand ideas. This is why the detection and dropping of labels is emphasized in this book. It is essential to peace of mind.

One way to lose harmful labels is to never battle against events which oppose what you want. Instead, look into yourself until you see that the desire was a vain attempt to find security by possessing people or objects. To accept things as they come does not mean the abandonment of your natural intelligence, but is the way to attain it fully. The secret is to blend and harmonize your intelligence with the whole of Cosmic Intelligence. And then you will discover no division in the two; you will see that you are Cosmic Intelligence.

When you place the true kingdom first, you can afford to ignore all else, which is precisely what makes all else right.

Dorothy S. always attended classes by herself. One evening she added this idea to the discussion: "You say we make our world whatever it is. Will you please explain a bit?" Reply: "When meeting someone, notice how his manner tells you how to handle him. For instance, you don't tell secrets to a talkative person. Next, realize that your manner tells others how to deal with you. This helps you make the connection between what you are and what happens to you. This leads to other valuable insights as to how you make your world whatever it is, which opens the door to a new world."

Everything you are asked to do for yourself is

in perfect accord with your reason and ability. Only falsehood is unreasonable and impossible. Your invitation to the banquet includes understandable directions for getting there. The necessary is always possible. From your present viewpoint you may be unable to see the Andes mountains, but they still exist. You need not make the slightest effort to believe in their existence; you must just start walking.

THE SUCCESS OF YAZID

There were once two Arabian boys, one named Yazid and the other named Haroun. They became close friends as they shared boyhood adventures in village and desert. But the passing years separated them, with fortune making Haroun a great sheik, while turning Yazid into a poor rope-maker.

One day while selling his ropes in a street in Baghdad, Yazid came face to face with Haroun. The delighted Sheik Haroun offered his boyhood friend a position in his court as the royal date merchant, which was accepted. Only the very best dates in the land were good enough for the sheik's kitchen, so Yazid's task was to find and buy only superior dates.

A week later Yazid returned on his camel with a load of dates which he believed were of fine quality. But when sampling the fruit and finding it inferior, the sheik's advisers wanted to discharge Yazid. But when hearing of it, Haroun gently shook his head. "You do not understand Yazid," Haroun told his advisers. "He has lived in poverty all his life, consequently he has no way of distinguishing good dates from bad ones. He truly believes he has a load of excellent fruit, but that is only because he does not as yet understand. We must be patient with Yazid."

Sheik Haroun then instructed his advisers, "Each day I want you to give Yazid a few dates for dinner. Start with a lower quality and gradually give him better dates. His own taste will then show him the difference. Then, I guarantee you, Yazid will bring us only the very best fruit."

The sheik was right. Because Yazid truly wanted more knowledge, he was soon able to see above his previous judgments. And then he served both the royal court and himself only the finest of dates.

Self-command creates true happiness

Truth patiently understands our lack of knowledge of what is right and what is wrong. It asks only our permission in order to lift us from one level of insight to the next higher level. Then, we do right because we know right.

It is your own feeling of rightness which finally delivers success. You can prove this, for in a moment you will read a ringing declaration by Epictetus. Observe your rising consent to the advice, "Man, if you are anything, both walk alone and talk to yourself, and do not hide yourself in the chorus. Examine a little at last, look around, stir yourself up, that you may know who you are." You know that is right, don't you?

Can you intuitively feel that all human schemes for human betterment are illusory and tragic? Can you sense that both sides of any human quarrel are equally wrong? Can you feel the existence of an original way of thinking which is magnificently above human schemes and quarrels? Feel it right now, for you possess right now the power to blast away tragic illusions, which restores restful realities.

Commented Ray W., "You say that both sides of any human debate are wrong, that we should take neither side. But if we do this, where are we, and how can society go forward?" Reply: "With the exception of science, society never goes forward; it only rearranges the chaos. Taking a side is like cleaning only one side of a dusty window and then wondering why you can't see through it. When you deeply see that both sides are wrong, which happens when you cease to identify with either side, a third way of thinking enters your mind. This third way is true conscience."

Why does a man continue to swing like a pendulum between excitement and depression, depending upon what happens to him? Because he does not see that this kind of excitement must always be followed by depression. It happens to him all week long and he never notices it. His consciousness of this false process would make him receptive to the true way, which includes self-command. Now he is happy with himself, and therefore his feelings are no longer at the mercy of exterior events.

It is not good fortune when external affairs go according to what men call fortunate, for by cosmic law they must swing over to what men call unfortunate. It is good fortune when there is nothing in you which labels events as either fortunate or unfortunate. Win internal freedom, for that freedom can look out at the external world with its own clear wisdom, which alone is good fortune.

A man may wonder how his awakened mind will handle the daily events which now bother him. In an awakened state he will not find himself in many of the usual bothersome situations, for it was his hypnotized mind which attracted the events in the first place. Other events do not become problems because his new mind does not see them as problems. A free mind has no enemies and therefore nothing to fight. The conscious mind knows the secret of *living impersonally*. Think about this phrase.

INVITATIONS TO AN INDEPENDENT LIFE

1. Self-independence creates authentic contentment.
2. Live from the inner to outer, not the outer to inner.
3. Our healthy aim is to make the unconscious conscious.
4. Be influenced only by your own inner light.
5. Overcome yourself and you overcome the world.

6. Enrich your future by enriching your present.
7. Discouragement crumbles before self-knowledge.
8. The self-unified man possesses a unique intelligence.
9. Whatever is necessary for you is also possible for you.
10. These teachings make you happy with yourself.

9

The Sure Way to Healing and Strength

THE NIGHTINGALE

The Emperor of China heard of a nightingale whose song was of rare beauty. Sending for the bird, he arranged for a concert in the palace. So sweet was the nightingale's song that the emperor honored it with a special place in the palace.

One day the emperor received a box containing another nightingale, a mechanical one, with wheels and levers. Richly decorated with rubies and sapphires, it seemed to sing as sweetly as the real nightingale. But a fisherman remarked, "There is something wrong with it, but I don't know what."

The mechanical bird became the object of adoration for the emperor and his subjects, while the real nightingale was banished from the palace.

One day, the mechanical bird broke down. All attempts at repair failed. After leading his nation in mourning, the emperor fell ill from grief. When he called upon the mechanical bird for a cheering song, it remained cold and silent.

Unexpectedly, the real nightingale returned to the palace, where his beautiful song quickly restored the emperor's health. The grateful and repentant monarch offered the nightingale a rich reward for its noble service, which was declined. The nightingale told the emperor, "Only let me sing for you as I please. And tell no one our secret."

Cosmic principles are your allies

This is the condensed version of the story by Hans Christian Andersen. Like all lasting literature, it is not merely an entertainment, but contains valuable lessons about the ways of men:

1. The emperor's attraction to the real nightingale symbolizes the desire of a certain part of us for the truth.
2. The rejection of the real nightingale in favor of the false bird shows how easily we fall victim to the glitter of artificiality.
3. The emperor's grief is similar to human breakdown when false supports collapse.

4. The emperor's restored health upon the return of the real nightingale shows how human health thrives when the real and the true are welcomed.

If you show a small child how to turn his head back and forth in order to see traffic when crossing a street, he will at first do it mechanically. He will move his head because he has been told to move it, not because he sees how his own safety is involved. We must grow beyond mechanical obedience to cosmic principles to see how they connect with our true interests, for then they become our active allies. On a hot day it does us no good to think about cool water; we must make the water part of us. Consciousness must replace mechanical thought.

Harry H., who represented an American firm in Holland, wanted to know, "What is meant by self-interest? We are told it is wrong to be constantly concerned with ourselves, but how can it be avoided?"

"There are two kinds of self-interest, one of them destructive, the other of supreme value. All harm ful self-interest arises from thinking wrongly about yourself, especially in the area of self-images. If you wrongly think you possess a self which is apart from the whole of nature, and which must therefore compete and fight with other people and events, you have destructive self-interest. And it is an exhausting fight which you cannot win, for there is no such self which exists apart from the whole. It is like fighting an imaginary ghost."

"Then," said Harry, "it is false self-interest to try to win over another or try to feel superior to him."

"Of course. Human superiority and inferiority exist only in illusion. If you see this, all attempts to attain superiority and avoid inferiority come to an end—and so do the pains connected with such futile attempts."

"And what about authentic self-interest?"

"It is always based on an enthusiastic desire for the truth, regardless of the number of self-images which must be sacrificed."

Nothing is more important than the study of our unconscious self-images—how we invent them, tensely protect them and suffer a thousand times weekly from them. True self-interest enters by seeing the trick we have allowed these false selves to play on us. Freedom then appears. If you live in a dangerously creaky house, but get rid of it, you no longer worry over its dangers, nor are you hurt if it is criticized. You are out of it. This is what esotericism means when saying, "To lose yourself is to find yourself."

THE TWO PHILOSOPHERS

Two casual acquaintances were traveling together down an unfamiliar trail through the hills. During their conversations, one told the other, "I am a member of some of the great religious and philosophical organizations of the world. You might even consider me something of a scholar in religion and philosophy. Do you belong to any organizations like these?"

"No," replied the other man.

"Also," the first speaker continued, "I frequently appear in public as a teacher and lecturer on religious subjects. Do you ever give lectures?"

"Never," replied his companion.

"I might also mention," the first man went on, "that I have many famous friends throughout the world. They are the honored authorities who help mankind to solve the great mysteries of life. Do you have any famous friends?"

"None," answered the other man, who then added, "by the way, does your philosophy tell you how to get out of these hills?"

"No,"came the alarmed reply. "Are we lost?"

"You may be," his companion answered, "but my kind of philosophy shows me how to get out of the hills."

How to attain total healing

We must be as practical. What good is it to be a nervous scholar or a frustrated hero or a miserable leader? The only worthwhile philosophy is that which shows us where to go at every step of the journey. That is the kind of philosophy you are now absorbing.

At a certain point a sincere seeker will sense the absurdity of his present attempts to find rest and fulfilment in worldly successes. That sensing is both a crisis and an opportunity. If the faint awareness of absurdity is not refused, it becomes his turning point. Now he is on another path, which has its own challenges, but he meets them with an entirely new kind of spirit. Now realizing that the old ways cannot lead anywhere, he feels a strange confidence which seems to arise from his own deeper nature. He feels that at last, however stumbling his first steps may be, he is truly going somewhere.

Society's schemes and psychologies can only aim to make a man as comfortable as possible in his prison cell. Esotericism can successfully aim to get him out of prison altogether. This is why English philosopher Francis Bacon urged men to see everything according to its true worth. Which has true worth—public applause or private serenity? Which has authentic value—self-conflict as a way of life or self-harmony as a way of life?

It is the truth that sets us free, and there are two forms of truth involved in the process of self-liberation. There is first the shocking truth and then the healing truth. This is the correct and the only order of procedure. If we will not face the shocking truth about ourselves we cannot know the healing truth about ourselves.

Don't do another man's work. It cannot be done anyway. Do your own work. We work for the other man when we mechanically quote his shaky opinions, when joining him in a supposedly noble activity with hidden selfishness, when we agree to reduce his anxiety by praising him. This sort of waste can only lead to psychological bankruptcy.

Work for yourself and you will be paid for yourself.

Suppose you see an apple hanging from an orange tree. It is not necessary to call in a botanist or a philosopher to explain the strange sight. You need only make a personal examination in order to see it as a trick of some kind. One of the great values of esotericism is its total independence of scholarly theories and confusing speculations. When we see the unnatural as unnatural, that is enough; the hoax and its mystery drops from the mind.

Muriel Y. said she realized how often her impulsive emotions blocked practical thinking. This realization in itself testified to her earnest self-study. She heard, "Yes, emotionalism is like eating chocolates when you need a complete dinner. But remember, emotions in themselves must not be condemned; they must be deeply understood. This turns them into energies for self-awakening."

THE HEALING POWER OF NATURE

The home of an authentic teacher was set within beautiful country of colorful meadows and rolling hills. One afternoon, when visited by a group of inquirers, he wished to impress a certain lesson upon their minds. Inviting them for a stroll, he pointed out the natural beauties of the countryside, including a quiet brook and a grove of hardy oaks. Upon returning to the spacious living room of his home, which was used as a classroom, the teacher made his point. "You have just enjoyed the natural beauties of this region," he said, "but perhaps there is something you do not know. It was not always like this, for this land was once the scene of a terrible battle. Years ago the region was torn apart by charging armies. But now you see what can happen when the past no longer interferes with the present." The teacher concluded the lesson, "If your life has been a battlefield up to now, your willingness to give up the past can begin your natural healing and restoration."

Make this experiment in self-transformation

Your aim is to think in a new way, a way which is free from associations with the past, free from demands upon the future. A student of esotericism asked his teacher what it meant to think in a new way, and heard this reply, "Think outside of yourself." You may wonder how you can possibly think outside of yourself, but it is no mystery. There exists a unique energy in every person which is *not* his habitual self. When this uniqueness thinks, the universe thinks.

Alert self-experimentation is the key to self-healing. A group of earnest people in Iowa carried out one beneficial experiment for an entire month. I will outline this experiment for your own self-transformation. The aim is to simply watch what happens when you drop a habitual reaction of some kind. For example, watch what happens inside your psychic system when you simply drop:

Nervousness over a forthcoming crisis
Resentment at being criticized
Guilt over a failure
Craving for social popularity
Doubt over ability to change yourself

Experiment. Drop all such negative reactions. Just drop them every time they appear. Watch what happens. For one thing, you will feel a vacuum. You can understand why. Because you empty the space of your habitual response, there is nothing there. *Do not think it necessary to fill this emptiness. Leave it empty.* Now watch what happens. You will feel something you never felt before.

What results from experiments such as this? Whatever is wrong is corrected. No exceptions. We win freedom from those haunting anxieties we rarely mention, even to ourselves. We look at life with clear and healthy vision. Harmful habits disappear. There is no worry over the future. We know what life is all about. Because we are right, our day is right.

Dean H., who had studied Eastern thought, spoke up: "Zen teachers say we have nothing to get, therefore our cravings are false. Please explain." Reply: "A mind with a certain thought projects the opposite of that thought, for example, a lonely mind dreams of non-loneliness, or a frustrated mind yearns for satisfaction. This division of the mind into opposite parts—loneliness and non-loneliness—is an illusion. A whole, undivided mind does not project anything, therefore it does not create false ideas about satisfaction, therefore it has nothing to get."

We do not use what we have. Our mistake can be reduced to that. We do not use what we have because we have not taken time to be aware of what we have. Socrates told a famous story about men in a cave who refused to believe in the existence of the outside world, which condemned them to misery. Walt Whitman invites psychic cave dwellers, *"Whoever you are, come forth!"*

To see how trueness and calmness go together, we can examine how falseness and nervousness go together. Because man fails to see his actual completeness, he assumes he has a self which must be made complete through pursuit, capture, possession. But since the assumption is false, he is putting money into a bottomless safe, which demands a new filling every second, much to his frustration. As he understands his original error, his desire for possession vanishes, as does his nervousness.

THE TROUBLED MAN

A man with a troubled mind went in search of a mystic master. After wandering around for several months, he finally found a mountain retreat where a teacher resided. The troubled man inquired, "Is there a special way to attain mental completeness?"

Replied the teacher, "Yes, a way exists."

"Please tell me about it."

"When you eat, simply eat. When you work, simply work. When you play, simply play."

"But," protested the man, "that is what all of us

do. Have I wasted my time in coming here? There is no difference in your way and the way of everyone else."

"There is a tremendous difference which you do not see."

"What is the difference?"

"When you eat you wonder whether your table companions like you or not. When you work you hope to be promoted above others. When you play you think it is necessary to play better than your friends. That is the big difference. On your way back down the mountain, think long and hard about this. You may then wish to return for a second visit."

Open yourself to a new healing

Man is unable to concentrate on what he is doing at the moment. His mind is forever wandering into the past or future or holding imaginary conversations or unreeling dramatic scenes or getting lost in complaint and depression and excitement. His mind is rarely at home with itself, which is why disorder remains. Solution: Come back to your own mind.

You do not have to wonder what is best for you. Wondering and planning and choosing are the acts of a divided mind which still wrongly believes in fulfilment through acquisition. The mind is not satisfied by getting something outside itself, but is satisfied only by coming together with itself. The terms of self-gain and self-loss have no meaning to a united mind.

The mind is attracted to whatever corresponds to its own conditions. Hearing this, one man smilingly commented, "That tells me something new about myself. I seem drawn to noisy activities." That man's insight can lead him toward the next helpful lesson in the course—the value of a silent mind. It is the silent self which attracts everything good for itself.

We can tell what we are like by noticing what impresses us. We are impressed by whatever resides on our own psychic level. It can be no other way, for we are our own impressions. Whenever we see anything, we see ourselves, as in a mirror. Are we impressed with another person's cunning self-interest which masquerades as generosity? Are we impressed by hearing that self-facing is not our doom but our healing? See the difference in these two kinds of impressions. We cannot see above our own present level, but we can open ourselves to a higher level, which permits that level to impress us with its power for healing.

Follow this carefully. Rightness is a single, whole virtue. Authentic rightness cannot be divided into opposing parts consisting of one rightness for you and another for me. Divided rightness is false, causing conflict. Therefore, whoever sees what is *truly right* for himself will not behave wrongly toward anyone else. He sees self-rightness and other-rightness as the same thing, also, he sees self-harm and other-harm as the same.

The tighter a man has chained himself with wrong

ideas, the tighter he will try to chain others with them. It is his vain attempt to feel secure in a like-minded crowd. His peculiar logic thinks his own chains will somehow feel lighter if others have the same chains. This makes him hostile toward any other prisoner whose sudden awareness of his chains makes him want to drop them. If a self-chained man would begin to set others free, he would also set himself free, for they are both the same wise process of "letting go."

There is a way to think in which misfortunes and regrets are not created. You are now investigating that way.

THE MAGNIFICENT VIEW

Two friends started up a mountain trail together. One of them put more enthusiasm into his step than the other, and so found himself several hundred feet ahead of his companion. Turning a bend in the path, the higher hiker came upon a magnificent view of the valley below. Inspired by the sight, he increased the pace of his upward climb in order to see even more. The higher he climbed the greater his satisfaction with the view before his eyes.

Glancing down at his slower companion, the advanced hiker realized a few facts about his friend. He knew his friend would also reach the bend in the trail where the magnificent view would appear. Then, his friend would also be filled with fresh strength and energy, and his pace would also quicken.

How love creates new energy

Natural law decrees, "Direct a little energy toward cosmic heights and you will win additional energy for attaining greater heights."

Sooner or later, for the first time, you will catch a glimpse of that *Something Else* you somehow sensed just had to exist out there. Now you know it exists, and nothing can ever prevent your complete union with this unique inspiration.

People wish to be inspired, but what is the nature of true inspiration? Inspiration is unblocked energy. Understanding does the unblocking, which releases energy and inspiration. True inspiration abides quietly, but also flashes out with special brilliance, as when we grasp a new truth for the first time. We must be careful not to mistake emotional stimulation for loving inspiration. Stimulation fades, for it depends upon something outside of itself, but inspiration is both its own energy and its own source of energy.

Morris S. commented, "What we call confidence is apparently not confidence at all, for it fails us as often as it seems to succeed. Please explain false confidence." Reply: "The thrill of having others agree with us or of events turning out as we wish are forms of false confidence. Peer closely and you will see anxiety crouching behind such thrills. True courage is the absence of false courage; true courage has no need to think about itself; it is confident because it has no need to be confident. If I am at home I don't need confidence for getting home."

Healing and Strength

Everyone has an abundance of natural alertness for succeeding at the inner task, but most people waste it fifty times a day. For example, people are very alert to the opportunity to criticize others and are equally alert to criticism of themselves. Wonders could appear by turning this alertness toward self-release. Give your alertness to this question: Why do you have more confidence in your enemy than you do in yourself?

Remember that all energy is a single, unified force. The energy which lifts your left hand is the same energy which makes a carrot grow. The power which whirls worlds through space is the same power by which you observe the mood you are in today. This vast energy is ready to renew whoever makes himself ready for it. We make ourselves ready by refusing to take pleasure in negative emotions, by wanting to know more about life than what we see on the surface.

Love is the full, free and uninterrupted flow of life-energy through your psychic system. It is a river of energy with no dams or whirlpools or broken banks or dividing islands. Love is oneness, wholeness, mental health. This free flow starts by first becoming aware of self-division, and then by dissolving it through spiritual insight.

Save vital energy by avoiding idle speculation. Speculation is like paying for an airplane ticket you may never use. Don't speculate on your chances for future success, don't wonder whether or not other people will like you. Replace speculation with attention to the here and now. Notice the thought that just passed through your mind, be aware of the tension in your fingers, see how frightened people really are. Eastern teachings stress the importance of correct attention, comparing it to a candle in the night.

When he asked for a few practical facts to keep in mind, Roy D. was supplied with the following:

1. Life-healing is possible to all who truly want it.
2. The mind can be used in a totally new way.
3. Learn to separate the counterfeit from the real.
4. Replace human opinions with spiritual facts.
5. Realize that the inner determines the outer.
6. Things go right when the mind goes right.

THE MAPLE CABINET

A man had a hobby of building special kinds of furniture for his home. One day he saw an advertisement which offered to supply the basic materials for building an attractive cabinet of maple wood. The advertisement stated that everything needed for the cabinet was packed into a single box, ready for assembly. Driving down to the store, he bought the materials and brought them back to his workshop to begin his pleasant work.

But pleasure soon gave way to bewilderment. For one reason or another, the parts did not fit correctly. Unable to understand what had gone wrong, the man fumbled around in frustration.

Then, when removing the last piece of maple

from the packing box, he noticed a small booklet which he had previously overlooked. It turned out to be the precise instructions for assembling the cabinet. With the booklet in hand, he understood just what to do, and he did it pleasurably and accurately.

"Have I overlooked something which could solve all my problems?" That is the intelligent inquiry which turns fumbling frustration to pleasant progress. Assemble your new life with the instructions in the following paragraphs.

The beauty of naturalness

An unhappy experience travels in one of two directions. It can find a cave in our psychic system from where it ventures forth every so often to attack our peace of mind. Or, it can pass completely through our psychic system to vanish, to no longer exist as a threat. Its direction depends upon the individual's level of awareness. Through self-insight we destroy the caves, after which unhappy experiences can no longer repeat themselves.

Can you see the difference between a mechanical reaction to an experience and a conscious and impersonal observation of the experience? If so, you can see a star which most men never know is up there.

Norman T. spoke up during a discussion: "Suppose I am criticized as being an artificial person. What right response would help me the most?" Reply: "Are you artificial? To examine yourself is the right response. If the criticism is accepted as factual, the result is more inner health for you. But if it is a fact which you resist, self-division deepens. If you truly have no artificiality, you have been working very hard on yourself." Norman smiled at the last sentence.

Study these ideas about naturalness:

1. Unnaturalness is an awkward thought or word or act which is foreign to our true nature.
2. Unnaturalness is unnecessary.
3. Naturalness and happiness are the same condition.
4. *"Whatever is natural is never disgraceful."* (Euripides)

An attractive statue is created by chipping away all the stone which is unnecessary. Attractive naturalness is what remains after we, as our own sculptors, have chipped away our useless exterior.

When you have separated yourself from all which is foreign to your true inner nature, anything foreign in the exterior world cannot harm you. Your own psychic health is perfect immunity from whatever is unhealthy on the outside. In this perfect health you can experience everything that everyone else experiences, but you are never disappointed or frightened. Why? Because there is nothing in you which corresponds to the exterior illness, therefore there is no invitation to it to enter. Health invites only that which is of its own nature. Health invites health only.

Healing and Strength

Suppose a man is wearing a heavy coat on a sunny day. The coat makes him hot and uncomfortable, but he carelessly forgets to remove it. This is the human situation. We need only remove our heavy and useless ideas in order to enjoy fair weather. We never need to create a sunny day, for if we are sunny, so is the day. Our own nature, whether pleasant or stormy, is the very psychological weather we experience.

The ideas we acquire can be classified in various ways, such as ideas which inform and ideas which guide. Here is an idea which can be classified as an encouragement: Where there is true receptivity, the truth always registers in the mind to do its healthy work, whether we are fully aware of it or not. This conforms to the cosmic rule: "Do what you should do, and what should be done for you will be done."

Receptivity can be defined as the act of listening without self-interference.

THE PATH TO HEALING AND STRENGTH

1. The real and the true are healing medicines.
2. Welcome cosmic principles as your active allies.
3. Self-experimentation is the key to self-healing.
4. When we are right our day is right.
5. Higher health comes by receiving higher impressions.

6. Your new nature does not attract misfortunes and regrets.
7. True inspiration consists of unblocked psychic energy.
8. Replace human opinions with spiritual facts.
9. Artificiality is a burden, naturalness is a delight.
10. Your inner health protects against society's disorders.

10

Let Your Emotions Supply Fresh Energy

THE STUDENTS IN THE STREAM

An applicant was accepted by a school of ancient wisdom, which revealed the secrets of human life to those who were ready for them. Arriving at the school, which was located at the end of a valley, he was welcomed warmly and given his room. The next morning he strolled around the grounds, enjoying the natural beauties of the valley. After a while, his attention was attracted by the other students who were scanning the stream which flowed past the school. Some of them were standing knee-deep in the water, apparently watching for something floating downstream.

When the new student asked what was going on, he heard the reply: "Our principal teacher lives high in the hills above this valley. Each morning he sends the day's lesson downstream, enclosed in a brightly-colored tube. Part of our work is to be alert for the lesson and catch it."

Be free of feeling rejected

Part of our work is to make our emotions work for us, not against us.

Self-awareness makes you feel much better. Why? Simply because you see something you did not see before. You see you were carrying an unnecessary burden called the "self." Your world changes because you change. You are your own world. You make your world whatever it is. Many people don't accept this because they think it is some strange or mystical truth having no relationship with their daily headaches. If they worked to see this, all headaches having a psychological cause would end.

Neil H. commented, "I have noticed how easily people feel offended—including myself! Please discuss this." Reply: "Feeling offended occurs when a fact threatens to destroy a flattering self-image. We wrongly fear we may lose part of ourselves if we were to lose this unconscious image, so feeling insulted becomes part of the defense. Drop defenses, let fact destroy fiction, and see how soon the idea of being offended loses its meaning to you."

Emotions Supply Fresh Energy

In itself, there is never anything hurtful or incredible about getting rejected. It is hurtful only if we think people and events must conform to our wishes. If we have concealed hopes and demands, we will have disappointments. If we have no unconscious wishes, disappointment is impossible. Besides, when someone rejects you or your offerings, you should shout for joy, for now you are free of him, and owe him nothing; you can be yourself, you can live your own life.

You have certain ideas about yourself which produce certain feelings. You may have the idea that you must appear successful and happy in the eyes of others. This idea must always cause striving and tension. Now, if you completely dropped the false idea that you must appear successful—*how would you then feel?* You would never again feel that life is a tense competition—for in reality it is not.

Liberated thoughts liberate the emotions. Among such freedoms are:

1. Freedom from feeling alone and isolated.
2. Freedom from harmfully feeling that wrong is right and that right is wrong.
3. Freedom from being betrayed and cast down by illusory hopes.
4. Freedom from painful impressions that we must be socially prominent and important.
5. Freedom from wrongly believing in the existence of powerful enemies who must be destroyed before they destroy us.

6. Freedom from the annoying feeling that we must account for ourselves to others.

THE MAN WITH THE SIGN

There was once a wise man who lived on the shores of the Caspian Sea. All day long people came from near and far to ask for his advice on their personal problems. One day a man struggled up to him with a large sign which was carried awkwardly in his arms. The sign read: *Here is a Very Important Person Who Knows What He is Doing Every Minute.*

"My problem, sir," said the visitor to the wise man, "is the terrible weight and irritation of this sign. Please show me how to carry it more comfortably."

"There is no way to carry it more comfortably," replied the wise man, "but you can drop it altogether, and must have the courage to do so."

At this advice the visitor's face flashed with hostility. "You don't understand," he snapped. "This sign has served me for many years by attracting money and honor and friends. You would be surprised at the great number of people who believe it simply because they see it. Besides, I am so used to this burden I would not know how to live without it. I came here hoping to learn how to keep this sign, while making it more comfortable. It is obvious, great teacher," said the visitor with sarcasm, "that you are not as wise as you think. I bid you good day." The visitor stumbled away with his heavy sign.

Emotions Supply Fresh Energy

That evening, the wise man taught his class of advanced students, "You can help only those who are ready to give up their illusions about themselves. Try to show people the terrible burden of their vanities. Those who will listen will change."

Decide in favor of yourself

Lorraine J. reflected upon her inner life as she worked in her small dress shop. One evening in class she asked, "I am beginning to see what you mean by false self-images, but will you please explain how they enslave us?" Reply: "It is like a hypnotized man trying to feed an imaginary horse. If we wrongly believe in our fictitious identity, we will also wrongly try to feed it with foolish ambitions, causing grief. Freedom occurs when the imaginary self fades through self-insight."

If you can read human faces you will read apprehension in them. Apprehension ends through insight. If you walk over rocky ground while wearing only one shoe you will be apprehensive at every other step. This is the daily walk of most people. They feel fine as long as their artificial selves remain unchallenged, but apprehensively realize there must always be the next rocky step. See that whatever happens to you also happens to the entire universe. The self which sees this is not separate from the universe, therefore there is no division and no apprehension.

An audience in Nebraska heard, "You can decide in favor of yourself or you can decide in favor of false personality traits which parade around as you. Can you see the difference? Try. Try to detect false personality in action, for example, in connection with suffering. By trying to understand why suffering occurs, a man decides in favor of himself. By using suffering to make himself the center of his own attention, a man decides against himself. Always decide in favor of your own life. No other decision makes sense."

We must approach truth with an honest list of our fears, for truth understands and accepts that, but it cannot accept mental forgery.

Never hide from yourself the way you really feel about someone or something. Make it conscious to yourself and do not feel guilty about it. Just look at the way you really feel, while considering it an intelligent exercise in psychic health, which it is. Any temporary feeling of discomfort should be considered as normal to the exercise, for it is caused by the clash between the conscious real and the unconscious unreal. Be active with this exercise, remembering that we are punished by whatever we hide from ourselves.

A love for self-knowledge can be aroused simply by glimpsing how a lack of knowledge keeps us in a cage.

Whenever you wish to do something in the spiritual life, but fear it may make you feel foolish or make you appear to be wrong in the sight of others, do it at once. This is the secret of liberation. This is true courage. It is our wish to appear right and respectable which alone is wrong. It is wrong because it perpetuates self-punishment. Have no hesitation in proving yourself mistaken, for each time you do you lose one minute of night-time and gain one minute of daylight.

Never mind how weak and ineffective your early efforts may be. Never mind how little you understand. Plunge straight into the center of all your thoughts, while being watchful of all that happens. This is doing what is right and best for you, even though you may not see it as yet. Just remember that your part of the process of self-change is to become aware of all that is going on. If you water the root, the petal will unfold of itself.

THE VOICE FROM THE CAVE

An ardent truth-seeker heard of a cave from which a Voice spoke out to those desiring help. Standing at the cave's entrance, the seeker asked, "What is Truth?" Receiving no answer, he repeated the question for three days and nights. On the morning of the fourth day the Voice said, "Very well. Your persistence has made you worthy of an answer, for the courage to continue your quest while fearing defeat was part of your test. I will now inform you of the nature of Truth. The Truth is like a harp."

"But what does that mean?" asked the perplexed man.

"Go into the village market place," the Voice directed, "and look inside the first three shops you see.

Then come back and tell me what you observed."

The obedient seeker reported, "In the first shop I saw nothing but pieces of metal. The second shop sold merchandise which resembled lengths of string. On the shelves of the third shop were pieces of wood of different shapes and sizes. But sir," pleaded the bewildered man, "what is Truth?"

"The Truth is like a harp," repeated the Voice. "Now you must go and discover what that means."

The seeker wondered whether his strange experience had made him worse off than before, nevertheless he sought the meaning of the message from the cave. He wandered for several months until one morning while resting in a rose garden he heard beautiful music from an approaching harp. Remembering how the Voice had compared Truth with a harp, he studied the musical instrument carefully as the strolling harpist passed.

Then he saw. The harp was constructed from the three items found in the shops—metal, string, wood. Then the light dawned. The seeker knew the nature of Truth. He reflected, "When man correctly combines all his inner parts, to end contradiction and to create unity, his life is beautiful music."

Live with these inspirations

Each man or woman must have a similar experience. His self-investigation must bring him together to create a psychological unity which produces life-harmony. Here are fifteen contributions to self-wholeness:

Emotions Supply Fresh Energy

1. Test every spiritual or psychological system offered you by inquiring, "Does it or does it not present the blunt self-facing required?"
2. The next time you feel disappointed at the way a plan turns out, ask how you would feel if you did not care how it turned out.
3. Find something in yourself which resents being humiliated, let it suffer complete humiliation, without complaining—then notice something different about yourself.
4. Think of self-work as the persistent and pleasant daily task of releasing yourself from yourself.
5. If you have only one ounce of courage or energy or skill, use that one ounce, and more will be added to you.
6. Meister Eckhart wisely pointed out that the only thing we have to do for our spiritual progress is the very next thing.
7. The understanding with which you take one experience will be a power in your next experience.
8. What do you suppose would happen to someone who switched all his demands upon other people toward demanding his own self-awakening?
9. If a man strikes a wrong key on a type writer, he does not blame his neighbor, but how seldom he sees the connection between what he does and how he feels.

10. A difficulty is approached rightly when you inquire inwardly, "How can I think about this in a different way from last time?"
11. Everything necessary to true happiness can be obtained, so it is essential to learn to distinguish between the necessary and the unnecessary.
12. Self-doubt exists because a man is split into dozens of conflicting selves, each with its own demands and aims, so self-certainty is the natural result of self-unity.
13. The reason the world does not yield to you is because there is no world *and* you, so true happiness is realization of your natural oneness with the world.
14. It is a definite sign of rebirth when one part of a man listens to facts which another part of him does not want to hear.
15. Truth extends many invitations, but none should be heeded more carefully than, "Will you listen?"

THE SPECIALIST

"The most difficult student to teach is the one who thinks he already knows what he is about to be taught."A teacher in a school for cosmic wisdom made that statement to the other teachers, who nodded in agreement. One of the teachers was assigned to specialize in helping this kind of student. He soon worked out an efficient method for handling whoever was sent to him. For example, on one occasion, three students stood before him to declare in turn:

"I already understand myself perfectly."
"I already know what life is all about."
"I already comprehend the nature of happiness."

Said the teacher to the first student, "If you already understand yourself, why do you have so many concealed conflicts? Self-knowledge ends conflict."

The specialist spoke to the second man, "If you already know what life is all about, why do you change your mind so often? A man who knows life has no such confusion."

The third student heard, "If you already comprehend the nature of happiness, why are you so unhappy? The authentically aware man has no unhappiness."

The students who permitted the teacher's challenges to fall on their humility, instead of on hurt feelings, soon saw the light.

There is a way back home

A teacher knows a thousand times more about a student than he can possibly tell the student at the start. Seeing the pupil's concealed confusion, the teacher knows a direct attack against it will only arouse hostility, thus severing communication. So the teacher explains by suggestions, hints, encouragements, with one aim—to help the pupil see for himself where he is going wrong. Seeing this, the pupil permits the lifting of the cover from his own inner lamp.

A student remarked, "You said we must come to a teacher in the right spirit. What is an example of a wrong spirit?" Reply: "A person will pretend that *he* has something to give to the *teacher.* To back up his performance he may quote authorities or mention all the books he has read. This is his ego's defense when sensing the teacher's true wisdom. The only way to approach a teacher is with your actual emptiness—which he knows about anyway. Now he can help you."

Man is like a lost child who is so tearfully frightened he cannot cooperate with those who wish to help him. His rescuers would like to assure him that all is well, that there is a way back home, but the child's terror blocks his hearing. The great avatars say to tearful mankind, "Did it ever occur to you that your problem itself is false, but you block your own understanding of this? Would you like to listen to the explanation?"

Do you know that you can hear with your emotions as well as with your mind? This occurs when you are presented with a statement you *feel* is true. Read this wisdom by Henri Frederic Amiel: "*It is not at all necessary to be great, as long as we are in harmony with the order of the universe.*" Is there not something in you which feelingly hears the truth of this? When a truth is heard by both the mind and the emotions we receive that rich result called *understanding*.

Emotions Supply Fresh Energy

Someone has hurt your feelings? Realize that another person can be cruel or stupid as a *fact*, but not as a *power* which can harm you. Separate the fact of cruelty from the power of cruelty, for these two go together only in wrong thinking. If you flip off the light switch in your home, you separate the fact of electricity from the power of electricity. Do the same flipping in human relations, and no one can shock you.

When a man has been hurt by someone, his first instinct is to strike back. But the man who wants to get out of the human trap will refuse this self-destructive response. At the instant of observing the temptation to take revenge, he swiftly turns the aroused energy into constructive channels. He becomes aware of how his hurt feelings tried to restore a sense of loss by hurting in return. He sees how cunningly negative emotions try to capture him. Such a man is melting his trap.

A teacher told the story of two men who came upon a mountain spring with water of unusual purity. One of the men tasted the water, but feeling nothing unusual in it, never returned to the spring. The other man, feeling the water's uniqueness, came back every day for refreshment. "Develop your perception of truth," counseled the teacher, "and you will be drawn to your own refreshment."

THE EXQUISITE APPLE

One morning a teacher of real knowledge wished to help his students to hurdle a particularly high barrier to inner advancement. Upon entering the lecture hall, the class saw their teacher standing next to a table. Upon the table was a covered object about the size of a large bowl. The teacher began his lesson with the following story: "There was once a man with an intense interest in growing unusual varieties of apples. He sent all over the world for trees producing apples of unique flavors and colors. By careful grafting and crossbreeding he found himself with a multi-colored apple of exquisite taste. No apple previously known by man had ever excited such delight as this one."

The teacher then described the apple in detail, telling of its many colors and rare texture. Then he said, "I have told you many things about this delicious apple, so your minds are now saturated with knowledge about it. But intellectual knowledge is not enough. In order to know everything there is to know about the apple, you must experience it for yourself." The teacher then lifted the covering on the object, revealing a basketful of the rare apples, which were passed around. The students tasted both the apples and the lesson.

The truth about human anger

That was how one teacher revealed the difference between *hearing about* a truth and *experiencing* it for oneself. It is very easy to be deceived into thinking that the memorized words about a higher fact are the same as living within that fact. We must break through the wall of words to the self-release found in personal experience.

Taking a truth on the surface of the mind is like watering the leaves of a tree instead of its roots. We may hear a helpful fact a dozen times before it penetrates to the deeper layers of the mind. For this reason we must never assume that knowing the words is the same as understanding the meaning. As a healthy mental exercise, try to feel a truth as well as think it. This introduces a totally new energy into the operation. Try to feel what is meant by, "You shall know the truth, and the truth shall make you free."

An explosion of understanding occurs when a fact in the mind correctly meets an experience in the outer world. Your mind may sense the folly of depending upon others for happiness, but this is not enough; you may still seek satisfaction from others. One day you suddenly lose the person you have depended upon, which brings distress. But this is a wonderful opportunity. You can connect the shocking experience with the fact that others cannot give you happiness, for your emotions also now see this. Now, your whole nature sees the folly of dependency, which does not cause fear, but provides true happiness.

Both wrongness and rightness can be clearly felt. By becoming aware of wrong feelings, we clear the way for right feelings. This requires an intense self-honesty regarding the actual nature of our feelings. One businessman experimented by observing his emotions when faced by antagonistic customers. Seeing how easily he permitted their unpleasantness to transfer itself to his own feelings, he worked at freeing himself. As he proceeded with a clear mind, and not with mechanical emotions, he succeeded in handling people calmly.

"I probably need frank counsel," James K. admitted, "I just don't understand why I am so aggressive and quarrelsome with some people. Can you provide a starting point for self-insight?" Answer: "Notice yourself at the instant of your aggression. You know very well that violence provokes violence, still, you go ahead. Do you see why? It is because you get an emotional thrill, a false sense of power at provoking others. You take this thrill as being the real you, which it is not, in fact, it injures you. We will go over this several times in several ways. You will see."

Have you ever wondered why human beings are angry so much? It is because anger provides a false feeling of life. Along with other negative emotions, anger supplies a fiery feeling of aliveness, of agitation, of having strong individuality. But to take this imitation life for true life is the great blunder of mankind. The imitation prevents the real. Simple logic proves that an angry man is not a peaceful and happy man. Start today to see the difference between a false feeling of life and true life, then choose the true.

ON THE CLIFFS OF ARRAN

When school was out for the day, a Scottish lad often helped on his father's fishing boat on the coast of Arran. The boy's task was to remain behind to tidy up the boat after the day's fishing, while the father brought his catch to market. The narrow path from the boat to home twisted through rugged coastal cliffs. At night the trail was cold, windy and the cliffs turned into huge and strange shadows. It was usually dark by the time the boy finished his work, so it was with pulsing anxiety that he began his hike home.

The boy said nothing about his fears, but his observant father told him one evening, "Starting tomorrow night, I would like you to try something different. On your way home, do not try to be unafraid. Do not try to escape your anxiety; not in the slightest way. You are to walk home while being just as fully afraid as you are. Give yourself permission to be afraid. But I want you to be alertly aware of your state. Watch yourself being afraid, without trying to do anything about it. Never mind if this sounds strange to you. Experiment with it every evening."

Following his father's advice, the boy experienced an interesting change in himself. By not trying to fight his anxiety, he began to understand it. For one thing, he saw clearly that the fear was in himself, not in the dark path. He continued to experiment. Then, one evening he felt a sudden explosion of understanding. He realized that he was no longer even thinking about whether he was afraid or not. That was because he was not.

How to make enemies vanish

Our aim is to understand the nature of fear, not to fight it or escape it. That aim is a sign of higher intelligence.

Ernest C., who was advancing rapidly in his esoteric education, came to ask a single question: "You say that all enemies are self-created, and that a willingness to give them up will make them vanish. May I have an explanation?"

"We must first understand how the mind operates. Ordinary thinking swings back and forth in opposites, between yes and no, left and right, friend and enemy. When you identify yourself with either side, you create its opposite. If you call yourself a success, you create a label called failure, which haunts you. Clear, so far?"

"Yes."

"This thinking in opposites is useful only on a certain level, for instance, when you say yes to a heavy coat and no to a thin one on a cold day. But spiritual matters cannot be understood with yes—or—no thinking; you must rise above both of them to a third way of thinking. This higher thinking uses no labels; you do not call yourself either good or bad, popular or unwanted. You have no identity based on either side."

"I understand," said Ernest, "but how does this dissolve enemies?"

"If you cease to identify yourself with one side of these opposites, the other side cannot exist for you. If you do not hold one end of a stick, the other end has no significance to you. If you do not call yourself a persecuted man, how can you have a persecutor? In this free state you are One with yourself and with everything else in life. Whatever is One has no split parts, is undivided, therefore, it does not have opposites or enemies."

"How can I personally experience this freedom?"

"Be willing to live without enemies. Give up the feeling of excitement they give you. At first this will make you uneasy, for your false self will miss the emotional agitation on which it thrives—and which it uses to make you unhappy. Give up one enemy a day, then a totally new experience will be yours."

Fear can be conquered, but you must rise up against it with tremendous emotion, then settle down to study and understand the entire process of fear. If you have a knotted rope you need only understand the knots in order to remove them. You know the knots have no intelligence of their own to resist you. So our aim is to understand ourselves. Understanding is everything. To pursue the truth, to use every event for self-awakening, to perceive what is truly best for you, to cherish simplicity and decency—all this indicates the understanding which removes psychic knots.

We must understand, for example, the nature of envy. An art collector is not envious of those who own copies of a famous painting, for he knows that only the original has value. But people envy the apparent happiness or superiority of others, never seeing them as the imitations that they are. It is strange how people persist in believing that others are happier than they are. When a man returns to his true nature, which alone has value, can he still envy mere copies of trueness?

If we have the courage to first see what we are doing to ourselves, we will surely advance to seeing what we can do for ourselves.

HOW TO LIVE WITH HAPPY FEELINGS

1. Self-awareness attracts harmonious feelings.
2. In this new way, life is no longer a tense competition.
3. To drop the false self is to drop painful emotions.
4. Have a great affection for these principles.
5. Resolve to understand and to build self-unity.
6. Turn your emotional energies toward self-awakening.
7. The truth invites us to listen with an open mind.
8. Understanding abolishes hurt feelings forever.
9. The self-new man has no enemies and no frustrations.
10. Realize how much inner wealth can be yours.

11

Adventures Toward Authentic Happiness

THE STRANGER AND THE SHEPHERD

A traveler through Asia was weary and hungry at the end of a long day. Glancing around, he found himself in a strange and desolate place. Food from his pack soon satisfied his hunger, then, lying down among some boulders, he fell asleep at once.

A passing shepherd noticed the sleeping stranger and paused at his side. "Wake up, sir," the shepherd called, while gently shaking the weary man. "You must not sleep here." The stranger awakened to hear the shepherd explain, "You are in danger by remaining here, for dangerous beasts roam this strange land at night. Come with me. I will lead you to safety."

Sensing the rightness of the shepherd's words, the traveler awoke fully and gratefully followed the shepherd to safety.

What it means to be free

The lessons:

1. In our psychic journey we must not sleep.
2. Esoteric truths are trying to awaken us.
3. Awakening leads us to a truly safe and happy land.

The truth that sets us free appears with right action. And what is right action? It is nothing more than to go through your day with a watchful mind which seeks to understand why your day unfolds as it does. A truth may not always be understood when put into words, but it can always be grasped when put into experiences.

Just as our physical parts are connected to make up a single body, so are our psychological parts connected to form a single psychic system. So when you succeed in one area you also touch other areas with success. If you succeed in a regular reading program, you also achieve valuable self-knowledge. If you perceive that esoteric thinking makes life make sense, you also perceive the folly of clinging to old mental patterns.

Remember, your aim is to see the difference between:

True interests and imagined best interests

The awakened state and the hypnotic state

Clear thinking and muddled thinking

Authentic happiness and artificial happiness

Conscious living and mechanical living

Always keep in sight the fact that truth is in *you*, not in an exterior source, though help can come through a teacher or book. It is as if you ask a friend to turn on his flashlight long enough for you to find your own flashlight.

We must remember what we can do for ourselves. We must remember that the self which takes challenges all wrong can be replaced with quite another self which takes everything all right. Said a teacher to a troubled inquirer, "First notice that your present solutions solve nothing. Then remember the existence of a higher mind which transcends all problems."

Refer back for a moment to the story of the stranger and the shepherd. Do you see an extraordinary fact here? All by itself it is enough to make us want to remain awake. It is this: By remaining awake we are not in the place where the problems are. We dwell in an entirely different psychological location where difficulties cannot touch us. This is truly a magic land, for we have no problems to solve because we do not carelessly create problems.

Problems connected with either commanding or obeying other people have no existence to the awakened man. These are man-made opposites based on tragic desire for either power over others or for the abandonment of self-responsibility through submission to others. The self-blended individual is above commanding or obeying in his inner life, just as a graduated student is above the rules of his former school. Absorb the full meaning of this and your relations with other people will he brightly new.

In thinking about these teachings, never stray from plain and direct logic. Do not get entangled in words and emotions. Here is good and direct logic: A man can have a thousand friends, but if his thoughts are wrong he will feel wrong. A man can have no friends, but if his thoughts are right he will feel right.

Asked Robert R., "How can we understand what it means to be inwardly free?"

He was told, "Try to see what freedom is *not*. We are unfree when worried, irritated, tense. Freedom exists when you are in necessary states; these negativities are unnecessary."

OUT OF CAPTIVITY

In an ancient time a group of friends lived in a certain area of a peaceful country. They went about their daily tasks with simplicity and contentment. But without warning their country was invaded by a militaristic nation. The friends were carried away and scattered throughout the hostile nation to serve as slaves.

The separated friends realized that a united effort was their only chance for escape, so they sought out each other. Quietly roaming around during free time, they kept their eyes open and asked questions. As friend searched for friend, some mistakes were made, and sometimes the task seemed impossible. But their passion for freedom drove them on until all the friends found each other. Combining their knowledge of the strange land, they agreed upon an escape plan. When acting upon it they followed a secret trail out of captivity and back to their former contentment.

The purity of psychic power

This story illustrates the inner process for self-liberation. Man must unite all the friendly forces within him, for together they can intelligently work out a plan for escape. These good psychic citizens have familiar names, such as Awareness, Sincerity, Naturalness, Daring, Perseverance. In the next paragraph we will see how awareness serves as a friendly force.

Impulsiveness is a major source of human problems and regrets. The cause of harmful impulsiveness is clear enough—unconscious and mechanical behavior. We do what we do because that is what we always do. Impulsiveness can be broken by becoming aware of its inevitable damage. Spend money impulsively and we wonder what to do with our useless purchase. Speak impulsively to someone and we wish we had not done so. Awareness of such uncomfortable results is practical wisdom.

By wisely observing our own actions we can use any difficulty to end the repetition of that difficulty. The very intention to use an unpleasant situation for more inner illumination is in itself a light-generating power.

It is self-unity and self-unity alone which provides natural power for contentment. We can grasp this better by examining false power. People have all kinds of wrong ideas about power, for example, they believe it means to dominate men and events with a dazzling personality or with great wealth. Like all false concepts, it includes its own punishment. The person wishing such power will fear he may not get it, or if gained, he will fear its loss. True power is, simply stated, the power of being one with yourself. This is truly the powerful way to live, for then you have nothing to anxiously chase, nothing which must be won. Reality has already won, and you are within it, changed and contented.

The change is truly miraculous, as we can see by examining the idea of patience. True patience is an absence of the need for patience. What is commonly called patience is usually a suppressed annoyance over the delay of a desired benefit. A self-fulfilled man seeks nothing, therefore even the idea of patience has no place in his psychic system. If our hunger has already been satisfied we are not impatient over a delayed dinner.

Be clearly aware of mistakes along the spiritual

path, but never allow them to feel important, for that strengthens them. Mistakes along the way do not destroy the rightness you have won so far. Dropping a diamond into the dust does not lower its value. Start again, right where you are, remembering your supreme task of working for yourself in every circumstance. Let everything else, including blunders, be as nothing.

Dennis C., a naval officer, asked, "Why do I fail in my present effort to uplift myself?" Reply: "Because if you accidentally set a mechanical clock at the wrong time it will still be wrong a day or a month later. A wrong clock cannot correct itself; something higher than the clock's mechanical nature is needed. In us, consciousness corrects wrong mechanicalness."

As the mighty Amazon River empties into the Atlantic Ocean, it creates a vast area of fresh water. The river's constant power keeps the ocean's salt water more than a hundred miles away from the coast. Psychic power released through self-insight has the same purifying effect. A man living within the flow of his own fresh nature cannot be affected by impure events around him.

WHY THE VASES WERE SMASHED

An ancient Persian merchant who specialized in vases wanted to know the secrets of life. Locating a wise man, he asked for help. The wise man instructed, "Go to the highest cave in the hills.

Inside this cave you will find several sealed vases. I have set down the secrets of life on some scrolls which are inside these vases."

Finding the vases, the merchant was dismayed to see he had to smash them in order to read the scrolls. While knowing the vases were of inferior quality, he still thought he might sell them for a small profit. But wanting answers more than profit, he smashed the vases and learned the secrets of life.

Where true love exists

Our willingness to smash self-images reveals the answers we yearn to possess. The following paragraphs will make this clearer.

Any person or event or idea which seems to confirm the imaginary existence of what a man calls his "I" is welcomed as being virtuous, correct, friendly and must therefore be protected at all costs. Any person or event or idea which appears to threaten this same false self is denounced as evil, wrong, hostile and must therefore be destroyed at all costs. Here you have the entire tragic history of mankind, and the story of daily life as man now lives it. Look into this with your own benefit in mind.

Perhaps you now understand the teaching, "Whoever loses himself will find himself." An example will help. When a man dares to end his demands upon the exterior world, he plunges himself into an inner crisis, for now he can no longer use the agitation involved in demands to feel individualistic, to feel "alive." But only by entering and passing through his inner crisis is his false self ended and his real nature revealed. Now reconciled with himself, now awakened, he sees the hoax he was playing on himself, and is forever free of its agony.

If you will stand outside yourself often enough and long enough, you will finally see you are not at all who you thought you were. This revelation comes as both an amazement and a delight.

English author Edward Carpenter tells of a dream in which a sea cliff, inhabited by strange monsters, was whipped by a furious storm. But when the storm passed, the monsters had turned into colorful rocks and gentle waves. The lesson is plain: Self-awakening shows us things as they really are. What man on earth could want anything but self-awakening?

Phillip H. asked, "How does self-awakening connect with self-forgiveness? They seem to go hand in hand. What is the true meaning of self-forgiveness?" Answer: "Yes, self-forgiveness appears with self-awakening. You then see that you do not really live in time, but truly live in moment-by-moment self-renewal. Then, you may remember past events where you acted unwisely, but there is no accusing sense of self connected with the memory. In other words, you are totally free from your past. Incidentally, self-forgiveness and other-forgiveness are exactly the same thing."

This brings us to the question of love. Love is not at all what it is popularly supposed to be. Only the person who has risen above an acquired sense of self, who no longer has an "I" which opposes another person's "I" is capable of love. Love exists only where there is no unconscious mental division into "you" and "I."

Love is not the losing of oneself in another person. That is merely escapism. Love is the natural radiation of our own healing, in which our own wholeness includes the other person, without thought on our part. The sun shines on everyone. However, an important point must be added here. Authentic love includes an understanding of the other person, based on an understanding of oneself. Love clearly understands the weakness and pretense in others, but does not condemn them in order to feel superior. The person who truly loves is never gullible, which keeps him out of trouble with others.

We must think and respond from our essence. That is what gives you something of your own, which no one can ever take away. Maybe you feel timid about letting go of your present ideas about yourself. Maybe you feel that their loss will somehow leave you with inner poverty. The exact opposite will happen; You will have eternal riches. A Sufi wise man explains, *"When the heart weeps for what it has lost, the spirit laughs for what it has found."*

THE SEEKER WHO CHANGED HIS MIND

A man came to a teacher with the plea, "Please let me become your student. Above all else I wish to understand the mysteries of life."

The teacher asked, "Are you willing to go through the training required of a student?"

"I will faithfully perform whatever tasks are required of me," the inquirer assured the teacher. "Only let me prove my earnestness."

The teacher nodded. "In that case, you may start by cutting wood for the fireplace, after which you can repair the roof and work in the garden. Later, you can prepare the meals and clean up the kitchen."

"That explains the duties of a student," said the seeker, "but what are the duties of a teacher?"

"The teacher sits around quietly and gives orders."

"In that case," the seeker spoke up, "please train me to be a teacher."

How to develop a new enthusiasm

Many people claim to have an earnest interest in self-rescue, but fall by the wayside at the slightest excuse. So sincerity must accompany the seeker. Happily, whoever wishes to increase his sincerity can do so. Such a person should start his morning with this reminder: "The way my mind works today will determine what happens to me and will also decide the way I feel, for either conflict or harmony." This enables him to see himself as the cause of his experiences, after which he will want only those experiences of true value.

"I don't understand," said Milton J., "why we must examine negative things like insincerity and anxiety. It is much nicer to think about goodness and kindness." Answer: "If you are lost in a jungle, do you dream about the pleasures of home or do you study the nature of the jungle itself? The answer to any problem is in the problem-maker himself, so self-study is authentic self-kindness."

A classic story from an ancient teaching shows how men go wrong without realizing it. Some monkeys in a zoo had been receiving three chestnuts in the morning and four chestnuts in the evening. They complained to their keeper about this arrangement in supplying their daily chestnuts. Their keeper agreed to a change by letting them have four chestnuts in the morning and three chestnuts in the evening. This made the monkeys very happy—for a while.

Because man rarely examines his inner condition he seldom notices that his exterior changes do absolutely nothing for his contentment level. Captured by the temporary thrill of a raise in pay or in meeting someone of the opposite sex, he is unaware of how he always returns to the same haunting heartache.

A man ceases to do a certain wrong when his increasing self-study shows him why it is wrong. It is not enough for his tongue to say it is wrong or for him to refrain from doing wrong for fear of punishment. His growing consciousness reveals that the wrong is wrong for *him* because it perpetuates *his* conflict and frustration. The first time this happens a new kind of enthusiasm enters, like the enthusiasm of a detective whose hard work produces a clue which he knows will finally solve the case.

Whatever is right in you has power over whatever is wrong. This rightness need not even be the dominating force; it can be as tiny as a sincere wish to explore your way out of the psychic cave. Have that wish and you will have its power. Be willing and you will be able. For example, when overwhelmed by confusion, your wise response can turn it toward self-change, just as a river changes its course when overflowing its own banks.

Self-change does not require the aid of distant and mysterious thoughts. It needs only those nearby and basic thoughts which we can think right now, such as:

1. Consciousness removes those desires which push us around so painfully.
2. Naturalness and relaxation are the same thing.
3. Return repeatedly to a truth which you wish were not a truth and you will soon be delighted that it is a truth.

THE CANADIAN

Some years ago there was a young Canadian who did not quite know what to do with his life. Deciding to build a future for himself in the United States, he roamed around the areas bordering the Mississippi River. He worked at whatever he found available, putting in time as a railroad laborer and as a farmer. Moving toward the West, he found himself caught up in the wild atmosphere of pioneer days. Again and again, when crossing the plains or the Rockies, he barely escaped bands of hostile Indians. One time, when seeking gold and silver, he was lost in the snow-heavy mountains, to be rescued only at the last moment.

All the time that Richard Maurice Bucke roamed through and battled with life, he was thinking deeply about certain matters.

Returning to Canada, Bucke studied medicine. His eagerness and skill in viewing all sides of man's nature gave him national recognition as a medical psychologist. But Bucke's esoteric explorations convinced him of the existence of a state within man much superior to that revealed by ordinary psychology. He called that state "cosmic consciousness." This inner illumination existed, Bucke declared, in Christ, Buddha and Lao-tse, as well as in men like Plotinus, Dante, Baruch Spinoza and Walt Whitman. Anyone reading the testimony of mystical literature, said Bucke, could easily become acquainted with what these unique men experienced. He highly recommended the books of Taoism and of Hinduism.

Richard Maurice Bucke himself became a different kind of man. Out of his uplifted mind and spirit came his classic book, *Cosmic Consciousness.*

Nothing can stop you

Bucke's book was not just a collection of biographies. It contained an inspiring message for the reader: Something entirely different can happen to any man who is sufficiently tired of his life as it is. Regardless of earlier years, anyone can proceed as if today is the very first day of his life.

There are many cosmic secrets which a man cannot be told until he is ready to receive them. When he is ready for great things, he will surely have them. The process starts when a man stops trying to change the truth in favor of letting the truth change him. He then becomes a psychic magician who performs the fine feat of turning painful puzzles into healing revelations. With this in mind, work with the following ideas.

Whatever happens to you is a single experience, a One experience. There is no you *and* the event; there is only the total experience which includes you in it. A man wears himself out trying to catch the bus in life until it finally dawns on him that he is the bus as well as the passenger. If there is no you *and* an unexpected event, conflict is impossible. Obviously, there is then nothing to anxiously pursue, nothing which you are frantically compelled to catch. It is like having a nightmare in which you try to fight your way out of a jungle, only to awaken to find yourself safe at home.

At a certain stage in our upward journey, a new revelation must enter us. We must see that intellectual knowledge has done its necessary work, but cannot carry us any higher.

Acquiring only a knowledge of facts is like studying geology in college for twenty years but never graduating into personal exploration of the earth's crust. Once seeing what must be done, we must do it. Lucille K. mentally sensed the folly of letting other people influence her. But full consciousness of her own intelligence eventually changed other-influence to self-influence.

Some day, the unimportance of everything but

cosmic consciousness will come as a deep realization, meanwhile warmly welcome those hints of it which come daily. Exploring sailors of past centuries could sense when they were approaching fruitful land as yet unseen. Brisk winds from the land carried to them the scent of shore and shrubbery. The fruitful life comes first as a hint, a flash, a sensing. It may come as a feeling that the old ways are simply not worth it any more. It may come as an impression that life has a deeper meaning which can no longer be ignored. But however it first comes, you sense your drift toward a tremendous secret.

Your wish to become a new kind of person is supreme, for nothing on earth has power to interfere with your wish for cosmic consciousness.

THE FASCINATING ROCK

A teacher in a large city entered the classroom one morning while carrying a rock about the size of a cup. Setting it in prominent view on her desk, the teacher went on with the day's lessons. The rock appeared quite ordinary to the casual glance, so the pupils showed little interest in it. But as the morning went on, some of the pupils became curious. One of them said to the teacher, "We are wondering about that rock. Is there something special about it?"

When the teacher asked everyone whether they could see anything unique about the stone, the students shook their heads. They then heard the explanation. "It may look ordinary, but it tells an exciting story, a story of millions of years ago. This is a fossil rock, found just a few miles from here. It was discovered in the excavation for a new building."

Upon noticing the rock's crust of sea shells, the class listened in fascination to the story of the fossil from the ancient past.

How to make fear fade away

When you are presented with a new truth, do not assume it is ordinary. Look for a hidden story, for it is always there. Say with Walt Whitman, *"I believe that much unseen is also here."*

Progress produces new feelings, like the feeling of a hiker who sees at last the view on the other side of the mountain. A feeling of the uniqueness of these ideas will appear, as will a sensing of their rightness and authenticity. Norman M. felt as if he had nothing to do but be himself, which aroused additional feelings of refreshment and relaxation. Observe your own feelings as they appear.

A tool can make an impression on any kind of material whose nature permits the impression, such as wood or rubber. To make an impression on hardened iron or steel is much more difficult. We have seen the nature of our task. It is to permit new ideas to make their impression on our psychic system. We must never be afraid to melt our hardness to permit new impressions to alter our nature. Each self-melting reveals that the new impression was not an enemy as we feared, but the friend we always wanted.

A man unconsciously fears that invading reality will displace something within him which he considers valuable. But before allowing this fear he should inquire exactly what he believes to be valuable. A deep investigation will cause astonishment, for he will see how much he values the valueless. He treasures the very attitudes which keep him in conflict, which separate him from himself. He may see, for instance, how his desperate need for approval makes him a gullible victim of other people. Beyond his astonishments are his authentic treasures of self-trueness, and the ability to separate the imaginary from the real.

A country dweller was visited by a friend from town. When dinner was served the host apologized for the lack of vegetables, explaining, "Instead of buying vegetables, I am now growing my own, so I am temporarily out." That sums up our inner task. Instead of living from society's ideas, we must live from our own. For a time we will seem to have nothing, but this period of emptiness is one of the great experiences of life, for it heralds the approach of what is truly our own.

Necessary corrections in your life can be made right now, right where you are. You don't need to go anywhere, you need not talk to anyone, you don't need time. Corrections are made within the present mind, for that is the only residence of the problem. If you go somewhere or do something, the mind is transported physically, but remains in the same place psychologically. The change you need is outside time and space; it is instantaneous in the here and now. Then difficult exterior conditions fall into line with your mental correction; they have no choice but to follow. It is like inharmonious musicians who instantly harmonize at the command of their director.

Ronald F., who owned a health food shop, came to class with his question written out: "How can we increase the quality of our aid?" He was told, "The quality of your aid is determined by your own self-work. You earn higher aid by making yourself ready for it. There must be something in you with the ability to recognize a higher truth when you hear it from a teacher or read it in a book. An owl knows another owl when it meets one."

REFLECT UPON THESE SPECIAL MESSAGES

1. Seek to understand why your day happens as it does.
2. Your higher mind transcends all problems.
3. True power is the power of being one with yourself.
4. As invented self-images disappear, contentment appears.
5. Love is a natural radiation of self-wholeness.
6. Think and respond from your own essence.
7. The wish for self-newness creates the needed power.
8. Think about what it means to live in cosmic consciousness.
9. Look for the deeper meaning in a truth you have heard.
10. Anyone's life-correction can begin at this very moment.

12

How the Inspired Life Comes to You

THE HONEY CAKES

Scattered throughout India were several schools for those who wished to become skilled in religious art. Students were taught how to express true spiritual feeling through painting and music and poetry. The schools were testing grounds, for only those who learned their preliminary lessons were permitted to enter the advanced school at Benares. So lazy and insincere students fell away from time to time, but those who persisted in their studies were treated to a graduation dinner. For dessert, the graduates were served special cakes, small in size and rich with honey and spices. Though wondering at first at the special flavor of the honey cakes, the graduates soon recognized and enjoyed the extraordinary attraction possessed by the dessert.

At the advanced school in Benares, it was necessary to eliminate unqualified applicants and impostors. So all applicants were served with tea and honey cakes, while the master teacher carefully observed an applicant's reaction. The teacher knew that only those who had acquired a taste for the special cakes could recognize and enjoy them. Unqualified applicants reacted with either dislike or uncertainty, which proved they had not graduated from the preliminary lessons. So it was the applicants themselves who either qualified or disqualified themselves for advanced teachings.

How to tell right from wrong

No matter how high we may think we soar in spiritual skies, a frequent return to solidly grounded principles is essential. Self-questioning is an effective method: "Do I really understand myself as well as I think? Am I using unpleasant experiences as lessons in self-elevation? How can I increase my receptivity to what is truly right for me?"

A student of higher truth one day asked his teacher about religion, wanting to know what it meant to be religious. His teacher replied, "If you want to know what it really means to be religious, it simply means to do something which is right. Do you know the heavenly pleasure in simply doing something right?"

"What is right and what is wrong?" That question has baffled men for centuries. It need not baffle anyone who really wants to know. Right and wrong can be accurately judged only by a person who has raised his level of being to a certain height. From this height of true conscience he knows the difference, just as an airplane pilot looks down and sees the difference between a forest and a desert. The world is chaotic because wrong-minded men try to judge between right and wrong. The man who truly knows what is right for himself will also know what is right for others, for they are exactly the same.

"I would like to see more clearly," said Shirley B., "how I can successfully combat the waves of grief in my work and at home." Response: "You don't have to combat a single one of them. You just have to be a self-reconciled person. It is important to work at understanding this. Each person must understand that the fundamental problem is the problem he is to himself. Why waste our time trying to keep a room from spinning when we should be curing our own dizziness? Just patiently ponder. Some day, you will see, and the storm will end."

If we have a picture measuring 12 by 16 inches, we can try to fit it into a picture frame measuring 10 by 14 inches, but no amount of forcing can make it succeed. They just don't match. But we can get an entirely new picture with the frame in mind, winning success, for now they are made for each other. When our forcing ceases, we find a perfect fit with reality, for we were made for each other.

As we become inwardly accurate, we know the very same things known by those who lived above the common level. Ralph Waldo Emerson proclaimed freedom through union with universal principles. You will have the same insight as Emerson. Leo Tolstoy urged men to see the horror of their lives as a healthy shock for self-awakening. You will know by personal experience just what Tolstoy meant. Universal truths come to all who treasure them.

Our task is to be right with ourselves, for then we are right with all else. Cosmic rightness is a single, magnificent whole. The following terms all mean one and the same thing: God, goodness, mental health, truth, decency, happiness, freedom, reality, peace, love, sensibleness.

"Be aware of what you are doing at the moment you are doing it," is the first and last instruction for becoming a new person.

THE ENJOYABLE JOURNEY

There was once a river with many attractive sights along both banks. Many people, each in his or her own boat, took the voyage downstream. While on the journey, one man found himself deeply troubled by something. Every time he saw an attractive scene he wanted to stop and linger with it. In some cases he even wanted to claim the attraction as his personal possession. However, since it was the nature of the river to carry him forward in its unceasing flow, he felt frustrated and irritable. Not only that, but his fondness for the familiar sights of the past made him suspicious and afraid of whatever was around the next bend in the river. His love for the known made him anxious toward the forthcoming unknown.

Finally, he saw his mistake. It came as he understood the nature of the river and understood his relationship with it. Since it never stopped flowing, he realized that he must not try to stop it, but must become one with it. He could enjoy the sights, but must not try to possess them.

So the traveler permitted his mind to become one with the natural mind of the river. He just let the water carry him forward with its own easy flow. With that understanding, with that blending, he enjoyed every minute of the journey.

How to attain self-release

The only rules we can follow are those of our own original nature. So self-blending is the same as self-release. Then we flow through life without strained thought and without anxious effort.

If there is one feeling shared by billions of human beings, it is the feeling of being in danger. A sense of physical danger comes and goes, according to a man's environment, but the feeling of psychological danger never ceases to worry him. The danger is illusory—but try to convince him of it! The "self" by which a man identifies himself does not exist, therefore there can be no danger to it at all. How can a man see this for himself? By releasing, as much as he is able to take at a time, his imaginations about himself.

A report to growers of olive trees stressed the need

for good drainage. Olive trees having poor drainage tend to be small and to yield inferior olives. The same natural law applies to inward cultivation. If today's impressions are not permitted to flow away, to make way for the new, the psychic system becomes stiff and restricted. We should never hesitate to let the new replace the old.

Clifton L. asked at a meeting, "Why do we get angry and upset when we don't get our way?" Reply: "We get angry because our claims to power are denied by reality. We have self-images of having authority, with all the rights of authority, and when fact exposes the fantasy, we feel frightened and persecuted. The next time this happens, use these facts in a strong effort to understand. Remember, these false claims to power are unconscious, so you will not even believe they are there, which is just why they are so dangerous. Expose them once and for all; don't remain a slave to anger."

People who are disinterested in self-rescue take a "no" from life as a harsh tyrant. Those who want to rise above themselves take "no" as a friendly guide for the journey. We learn from "no," not from "yes." Reflect upon this principle, then use it on every occasion. A small victory in this is great victory, for it represents a breakthrough in fixed ideas; it signals the start of self-release.

Do not let a thought vibrate you. Mental vibration is not happiness, as it appears to be, but self-injury. If you spent ten years grasping this single truth it would be the ten best years of your life. Thought-vibration is just that—vibration over winning a success or over a thrilling memory or over a hope of future reward or over hearing gossip. Refuse this artificial pleasure. Instead, let these thoughts pass out of your mind the moment they try to make an appearance. This is moment-by-moment self-renewal.

There are a thousand reasons why the inner adventure is all that matters. For one, it is the only activity in which there can be no regrets.

THE PYRAMID OF CHEOPS

A group of American tourists visited the pyramid of Cheops at Gizeh. For an hour they walked around and gazed upward at the largest pyramid ever built. When returning to their hotel, they began a lively discussion about the stone giant. Each visitor mentioned the single strongest impression he had received by viewing the pyramid.

"I am impressed by its gigantic size," volunteered one woman.

"It is an engineering marvel," said a man, "considering the primitive tools they had in those days."

"To me," commented another visitor, "it is interesting to see how it has retained its original shape, in spite of attacks by time and weather."

A fourth member of the group was asked for his single greatest impression. "I am impressed," he said, "by the fact that it *exists.*"

Twenty-five enlightening points

This is what we are doing—permitting ourselves to

be impressed by the existence of a totally new way. Let the following teachings add to your impression.

1. Very often, the first instruction coming from an authentic teacher is the invitation, "Will you begin to question your life as it now exists?"
2. The two facts, that man dwells in psychic sleep but can awaken through right self-investigation, are the two most important facts about human existence.
3. When knowledge of human weakness combines with knowledge of spiritual strength, a third force appears, causing an explosion of consciousness.
4. When self-division is recognized and conquered, all other divisions and competitions, interior and exterior, cease to exist.
5. Faithfulness does not mean loyalty to doctrines or causes or persons, but loyalty to your own original nature.
6. When we know what to *be*, there is never any problem about what to *do*.
7. As part of your study of human ways, remember that mere contact is not the same as communication, for truly communicating people must have a measure of cosmic consciousness.
8. New life will come if only we will give up our imaginations about its nature, for imagination can only reproduce the old, thus preventing the new.
9. Once you set out on the path, you must never look

back to see how many other people are going with you.

10. In the cosmic world, anything you do not own personally you own abundantly, for it is not limited by a personal self.
11. It is only the self-organized person who can wisely and easily escape the snares and pressures of organized society.
12. We stay out of trouble with others only as we learn to stay out of trouble with ourselves, for both operate on the same psychological level.
13. New insight appears to whoever temporarily forgets his relationship with the outer world to inquire, "What is my relationship to myself?"
14. The acceptance of ourselves into sunshine or the rejection of ourselves into shadow does not exist outside ourselves.
15. Your true nature always knows whether counsel from others is true or false, sensible or nonsensical, which is why your first task is reunion with your original self.
16. Truths blossom in the mind according to the liberty permitted to their roots, just as flowers are more abundant in a garden than in a root-confining box.
17. A teacher inquired of a student, "Can you see the difference it would make if there were only one person within you?"
18. The present cannot and will not conform to the past, but it can and will conform with *you*,

for you and the present moment are always together in freedom.

19. It is good to ask questions about life, but having asked, remain silent and do not permit the surface mind to supply an answer, for this permits the whole of life to answer.
20. It is our own agreement with spiritual light which permits it to grow, just as firelight thrives by agreeing with surrounding oxygen.
21. A tremendous experience comes to whoever will carefully explain to himself, "True religion is what appears all by itself once I have faced and dissolved my unconscious negativities."
22. By discovering who and what you are at this present moment, you end the need for wondering who and what you will be in the future.
23. The truth can cure man because it is not impressed by man-made titles and reputations.
24. The unknown is merely something not yet understood, which is the only attitude needed while adventuring toward it.
25. It is a fact that the truth shall make us free, and an equal fact that freedom shall make us true.

A GLASS OF WATER

A teacher in an esoteric school invited his class to ask questions about the day's lesson. One student raised his hand to ask, "You say it is entirely possible to retain peace and self-command regardless of what happens to us in the exterior world. How is this possible?"

The teacher took a glass of water and poured it into a nearby vase, then poured the water from a vase into a cup, and finally poured the water into a jar. The teacher explained, "This water has found itself in a glass, a vase, a cup and a jar, all of different shapes and sizes. Regardless of its exterior container, the water retained its original nature; a container had no effect on it whatever. So it is with you. Realize your true and original nature. With this realization you will retain peace and self-command wherever you may find yourself."

A study group is valuable

Everything that happens to us falls on one of two parts within us:

1. Understanding
2. Resistance

Falling on our understanding is the same as falling on our essence, on our originally pure nature. This is the receptive center which prefers truth above all else. Falling on resistance is the same as falling on acquired opinions and habits. This center does not know what life is all about, but fearfully and frantically insists that it does.

Through honest watchfulness of our daily reactions we can easily tell where they fall. When falling on resistance, we suffer, either consciously or unconsciously. When falling on understanding, an event is met and passed, leaving us in quietude.

From this day on, let events fall more and more upon your understanding. One way to do this is to live above the level of descriptive words, such as winning and losing, generous and selfish, superior and inferior. A man who really knows what life is all about does not permit mere words to set off an automatic reaction within him.

The answer to any human question dwells above the level of the question itself. This means we must ascend to the height of the answer, and not expect it to descend to us. Sometimes we may take actions which seem right when doing them, but later discover more stones than silver. How can we find an answer to this perplexing question? Like this: If we will do things without assuming we know why we do them, we will eventually understand our actions, which will be right actions. Dropping the useless weights of false assumptions enables us to rise to the level of the answer. You can pick the topmost apple by climbing to the topmost branch.

Jeffrey M. said, “I want to understand why people behave as they do. You say that self-understanding must come first. Will you please explain?” Reply: “Suppose you own a copy of a certain book. Thousands of other people also own copies of it. Study of your own copy reveals exactly what it contains, therefore you also know what is in the other person’s copy. By seeing our own thoughts and motives, we perceive the thoughts and motives of others. This makes us wise and efficient in dealing with people. Self-study makes you a mind-reader.”

You may wish to join or start a study group which discusses these teachings. The group need not be large or tightly organized. If only a few people come together with a deep desire to break out of themselves, the psychic bars can fall fast.

A study group should keep the fundamental principles foremost. One class in New York used the following principle as the evening's theme: *"There is something within every man which wants to help him, enlighten him, make him succeed with a new life."* This resulted in a helpful session centering around the topic of unseen and unused inner forces.

But whether you work with others or all alone, your association with esoteric ideas is an authentically thrilling experience. It is like realizing for the first time what a big place the sky is.

THE PATROL

The supervisor of an immense national park in Africa was given the task of training new members for the park patrol. On the first day of instruction he began his class by providing general knowledge. The recruits received basic information for patrolling and protecting both the human and animal populations of the region. The supervisor then imparted specific instruction by saying, "When you are in the jungle or on the grasslands, success depends largely upon your sense of hearing. Be alert to various sounds at all times. Listen as if there is something there you do not as yet see."

The supervisor explained his advice, "Become

aware of the sound of an approaching storm, of the growl of a dangerous animal. Also notice friendly sounds, including the trickle of an unseen stream, or the call of a rare bird we may be seeking. Alertness to the sounds around you can prevent problems from arising, also it guarantees your own safety wherever you patrol."

To deepen the impression on the recruits, the supervisor concluded the day's class by repeating an earlier statement: "Listen as if there is something there you do not as yet see."

Your life can be totally different

For those who want a different life, there is no better counsel than, "Listen as if there is something there you do not as yet see." Whether reading an esoteric book or attending a truth lecture or experiencing life from morning to evening, that can be our cheery aim. There *is* something there we do not see, which alertness will reveal. We might finally realize how defensiveness prevents learning; how it stands as a wall between us and the breezes of truth which seek to refresh us. We may understand that we do not lose ourselves by abandoning acquired and useless beliefs, for we are no more our beliefs than we are an acquired table or chair. We may see how unwanted habits cease to renew themselves when we no longer give them false value, just as weeds fade when no longer watered.

"Over the years," remarked Alex G., "I have followed various religions and teachings, but everything remains the same. What is wrong with my plans?"

Answer: "Try to see that this is not the way things work. If you could see just that much—that the way you presently work is not the way *it* works—the revelation would instantly change your direction. This new direction leads toward self-newness."

Realize the existence of a new kind of power, of a completely different way of taking daily challenges, of a delightfully original form of life. They exist for you and they exist at the very instant you read these lines. They are yours for the loving and for the inviting.

All along the path we meet so many things to wonder about. Our wondering must be turned toward the right direction. "Is there a higher way than my present way?" is healthy wondering. "Do I have confidence enough to continue with my journey?" is useless wondering. If you have no confidence in yourself, proceed without confidence, which is perfectly possible.

Has it ever occurred to you that you have never before occupied the exact moment which you occupy right now? And do you see what this means? Do you catch a glimpse of your liberty? Think. When a room in your home is completely emptied of its old furniture, you can furnish it in any new way you wish. The very emptiness of the room is your opportunity. If the present moment is emptied of yesterday's accumulations—which in fact it always is—you can do with it whatever you wish. Yesterday can neither restrain nor influence you. The freedom of each new moment is your ever-new freedom.

ACROSS THE LAKE

A young man found a new home for himself on the shore of a large lake. The easiest way to reach the village on the opposite shore was to sail straight across the lake itself. He purchased a small sailing boat and set out for his first voyage to the distant village. But unexpected and baffling winds carried him off course so often he felt it best to return home, which he did. Additional attempts also failed. In spite of earnest efforts, he was carried away each time by the puzzling breezes.

Realizing his need for advice, he asked a boating expert, "How can I prevent the winds from carrying me off course?"

The young man heard the expert counsel, "Study your boat, part by part. Understand the relationship between sail and wind. Notice how the slightest shift of the rudder affects your direction. The relationship between boat and nature is actually harmonious, but you must learn how to harmonize. Then you will be in command of both boat and weather; you will not be carried away by every passing breeze."

Let your inner adventure be supreme

It is not necessary for anyone to be carried away by worried thoughts or vague hauntings or anything else contrary to cosmic consciousness. Awareness of how we are carried away is the beginning of self-knowledge which ends the tyranny of inner negativities. Now we are wisely transferring control of our lives from the fickle winds of fate to the royal influences of our true nature.

Words, which have powerful influences, can serve as tools for inner correction. Take a person who has strong convictions which keep him tensely defensive or which cause embarrassment when he is proved wrong. This person could begin to say to himself, "According to my present viewpoint I think I should take this action," or "According to my present viewpoint I believe we are right and they are wrong." The phrase "present viewpoint" leaves his mind wide open to future thoughts which may be far superior to his present ones.

Michael W. explained, "I want to escape my psychic jailers like anxiety and depression, but I don't know how. That is the whole story—I simply don't know how." Michael was told, "You know more than your jailers. Of course you do. Listen to what you already know within your own self. The insight is there all right but you have never given it deep and consistent attention. That is why you are here in class—to listen to your original intelligence which knows everything you wish to know."

It is, of course, the Truth that makes us free. Truth is that which is:

Without illusions
Factual
Effortless
Truly right
Without labels
Harmonious
Undivided

Eternal
Pure
The only Power

The best way to untwist a tangled cord is to hold one end and let the other end swing freely. Having nothing to prevent it, the cord unravels of itself, returning to its normal condition. Likewise, when we learn to swing freely, without artificial securities, natural contentment returns of itself. The difficulty with swinging is our fear that we may fall out of our usual shape, but falling is precisely what must happen. We are afraid only because we cannot see beforehand that we eventually fall not into a jungle, but into our true psychic home.

A guest at a country estate was about to drive back to his home. His host gave him instructions for avoiding the pockets of fog which invaded the area from time to time. "Follow this route," assured the host, "and you will never be overcome by fog."

Our original nature speaks with just as much assurance. We then prove its accuracy for ourselves, for we travel the clear road.

VALUABLE TRUTHS IN REVIEW

1. Think about these fundamental facts constantly.
2. Self-reconciliation cures all our daily difficulties.
3. The inner adventure will never cause regret.
4. The very existence of truth is a tremendous truth.
5. Be loyal only to your original nature.
6. Agree with the healing facts which approach you.

7. Let each event in life fall upon your understanding.
8. Learn how life truly works, then follow it.
9. Every new moment is a fresh opportunity for victory.
10. The truth is eternal, pure and the only Power.

ABOUT
NEW LIFE FOUNDATION

****

New Life is a nonprofit organization founded by Vernon Howard in the 1970's for the distribution and dissemination of his teachings. It is for anyone who has run out of his own answers and has said to himself, "There has to be something else." These teachings *are* the something else. All are encouraged to explore and apply these profound truths—*they work!*

The Foundation conducts classes on a regular basis throughout Arizona, Colorado and Southern California. They are an island of sanity in a confused world. The atmosphere is friendly, light and uplifting. Don't miss the opportunity to attend your first New Life class.

For details on books, tapes and classes write:

Headquarters

NEW LIFE FOUNDATION

PO Box 2230
Pine, Arizona 85544
(928) 476-3224

Web: www.anewlife.org
E-mail: info@anewlife.org

Vernon Howard, Founder

TELL A FRIEND!
SEND US NAMES

April 17, 2016
8:30AM

Notes

Just feeling hopless - I want a job the one in the Marina - At least A place where I am LOVING the location & able to attract the things I want - April is a time of transformation - I hope so!

- DSW - return shoes
- Mail headshots
- Study @ C/B
